Practical Leadership

Making a case for Synergy

David "Ricky" Sobrino

Copyrights

ISBN: 9781078134705

EAN: Not Available

Mama',

Tan cerca de tu meta, tuviste que soltar tu batón.
Yo no lo he olvidado. Contigo en mi corazón,
terminamos esta meta juntos.

Table of Contents:

Preface and Caveats

Preface.

There are multiple purposes for this book. The brief explanation of these purposes comes down to two words, advocation and application. First, I will try to advocate a leadership definition based on the concept of synergy. Secondly, I will endeavor to apply this new definition of leadership in a practical way. This application will assert how synergy plays a part in relation to a variety of commonly understood concepts of leadership.

This book is constructed as a practical tool. By design, it wishes to simplify and yet amplify the use of leadership. Whether you are a leader, a student of leadership, someone wishing to become an effective leader or a follower; this narrative will help you understand practical uses of leadership. It does so by defining in a utilitarian way, the concept of leadership. This definition is meant to enhance your abilities as a practitioner of leadership towards the success of your organizational goals.

One main reason for writing this treatise was the general realization academia does not have a unified or simplified definition of leadership. The understanding of leadership which is pursued by academia includes leadership centric research at universities as well as industry-wide think tanks. With all this research, academia struggles with a practical and fully encompassing definition of leadership. The issue with academia is not the effort in research, leadership is well studied. Yet, a problem surfaces when academia tries to find a common starting point to describe, analyze and conclude

5

any leadership centric discussion. Depending on a point of view, leadership can mean different things to different individuals. Thus, if a solution to any organizational challenge is to be found in leadership, then at the least, a commonly understood starting point is required. One goal of this book is to produce a leadership equivalent of the "starting point" of a leadership centric discussion.

Thus, this project seeks to inform and guide actions to enhance the concept of leadership. It is worth noting this discourse assumes leadership to be a positive activity of human affairs. The direct recipient of leadership actions are the team members associated with the stated goal. If actions under the disguise of leadership effect negative outcomes to team members, then the leadership framework applied was not by definition a true leadership scheme. It is most likely despotism. It is hoped this book points and guides the reader to a leadership framework which is very positive for the team members, the implicit stated goals of the effort, and the leader(s) as well.

Caveats.

Except for the beginning of Chapter 1, the writing is mostly in a third-person narrative format. Chapter 1 will describe my experiences as a leader. These experiences combined with study and analysis (i.e. trial and error), have culminated in the forming of a practical definition and application of a leadership framework. There are a great number of books and articles in which leaders describe themselves and their leadership styles. This narrative is different. It will start with a definition of leadership, and then attempt to apply this definition to known leadership constructs. In this book, the term constructs are meant as the framework or environment of a leadership effort. Furthermore, this book predisposes heavy favoritism to group goals, the team members, and the system which can create success. The

6

author is of little to no consequence. You will find as you read this text the common idea of centering leadership constructs on team members and the organizational goals. Thus, this book de-emphasizes the role of the leader in favor of the system which yielded success and the team members who made it happen. True leadership outperforms and outlives any leader.

Could you use a simple case in point? Credited to U.S. President Harry S. Truman, President Truman articulated ... "It is amazing what you can accomplish if you do not care who gets the credit." Enough said.

Please also note this work is not intended to be primarily academic. This book will cite and credit direct concepts to the authors who discovered or reviewed the data. This is done to maintain scholar integrity. The general idea is not about "reinventing the wheel" either. This work attempts to specify what "wheel" are we talking about, and what is the best way to use its' attributes.

Finally, please note this book is mostly secular in nature. However, as it will be stated in the acknowledgment section, I profess to be a Christian. I make no apologies for my faith in Jesus Christ. Whether the moral tenets of the Christian faith are practiced or understood by the leadership practitioner, it is not the intent of this discourse to preach or coerce Christian thought. However, the Christian Bible is full of tenets applicable to the leadership construct. When such biblical examples are described, these will be appropriately cited. It would be hypocritical for me not to give credit to Him who put it in my heart and mind to write this book. I pray and hope this writing will help the reader achieve a successful application of the concept of leadership in their professional and personal affairs.

Chapter 1

Leadership: A Different Definition

Leadership, what's up with that!?!

Why Leadership?

It all started with a question: *"Why do they yell so much?"* This question was posed by a 12-year-old curious pre-teen when talking to the former United States Marine Corps Captain Ernesto Lluesma, the husband of my mother's best friend and colleague. Enthralled by war movies at the time, this young boy did not understand the need for an un-gentile demeanor from military officers/sergeants giving orders. To this preteen, there seemed to be a lot of yelling for no apparent reason. With kind patience, Captain Lluesma tried to explain leadership and discipline to one who had none, nor understood either. He explained the need for a concerted effort in unity to achieve the expected mission. However, comprehension was not achieved. How could it? The young boy needed to understand a complex set of human interactions (leadership). This would take years for him to absorb. Yet, there was one thing achieved in these conversations (as this inquiry was repeated more than once). As I grew older, I decided to study and use leadership as a cornerstone of my professional and personal life.

After obtaining a bachelor's degree in Hospitality Management, I was hired as an entry-level manager at a resort hotel. In this experience, I quickly learned one of the first lessons in leadership. At the undergraduate level, leadership was taught as an attribute of a good, or successful manager. Undergraduate Hospitality academia did not specify what made good leadership practices other than to use leadership as a precursor to motivating productivity. The manager would explain (or was made to understand by the executive hierarchy) what was the generally expected outcome of the team. The manager then assessed and assigned the available assets to meet the goal provided. Leadership was tantamount to conjuring subordinates to do their respective jobs. The manager was expected to produce team member cohesiveness, but there was no model to assert this enterprise. In this environment, the need for success (or goal achievement) was clearly understood, but not how the goal was to be achieved. Modest success was achieved, but the methodology on how it was achieved eluded me. Maybe Captain Lluesma was up to something.

At the resort hotel, there were "dark clouds gathering." A poor leadership climate would soon exacerbate its' dissolution. The flawed environment which ended in failure was unique. The hospitality management chain where I worked was a part of a real estate centric venture. It became very clear to me the realtor centric investment approach to the business model might have been excellent, but the operational functionality was lacking. This is to say the parent company was excellent in finding great hotel/resort properties and procuring them. But they were very deficient in operating the acquired properties. As I grew tired of the shortcomings of upper hotel management regarding basic management systems, I chose to make a drastic career change. Inspired by my brother, a United States Air Force (USAF) lieutenant, I decided to join the USAF. This was a good call for many

9

reasons, one of them being the bankruptcy four years later at the hotel chain I worked.

Throughout my 20-year career in the Air Force, which afforded me plenty of leadership opportunities, I honed skills in which I was able to extract a definition of practical leadership. In part, this was due to the fact the USAF begins leadership training little by little, from a junior officer up to command opportunities in higher ranks. As a junior officer, I was exposed to followership (as a lower-ranking officer) and then leadership, (notably as a unit commander of a small flight operations unit). In the Air Force, you are never too far from the follower dynamics (being around junior officers, sergeants, and airmen), at the same time dealing with leadership among higher echelon officers (commanders, etc.). These practicums were essential for my understanding of leadership. The chats with Captain (Don) Lluesma began to ring true to me. It was in the military where I began finalizing the idea of a synergetic approach to leadership. After retirement from the Air Force, my next employer gave me the opportunity to explore where the central theme of leadership is anchored.

After my military career, I joined a sizeable large freight operation as a pilot and now find myself flying as a Captain. The pilots of this flight department come from three drastically different leadership models: ①, purely military, ②, purely civilian flight operations background ③, a hybrid of both military and civilian backgrounds. With this menagerie of experiences and expectations, the use of synergy as a component of a leadership model has been crucial. Foremost, leadership in the cockpit is crucial for safe operations. Using a cooperative leadership model enhances the experiences of all crewmembers to make sure the right course of action is taken. This is accomplished in the best interest of safe operations, regardless of how or who was the leader or impetus of the

actions. Thus, leadership has become a crucial day-to-day aspect of my professional life.

With all these experiences, leadership has consumed most of my thought processes. Just about every day I try to apply, study and dissect the leadership actions around me. Leadership is complex, yet simple. Leadership involves various disciplines and artful execution. I have learned at least one thing for certain about leadership: it is an integral part of our lives. **Leadership is a fulcrum of the human experience.** The understanding of leadership is necessary to assert any human-directed collective solution. When two or more individuals coordinate any action, a leadership construct is used. This is true in any relationship or environment. The requirement is simple. You need two or more individuals and a specific coordinated goal. Thus, leadership needs to be understood in order to reap the benefits of its' use. Leadership affects us all, and if employed correctly, it should benefit all of us as well.

So, what is Leadership?

Good question! However, as alluded previously, the answer to this question is just as easy as explaining poetry, beauty, or even complex theoretical physics. Our understanding of the definition of leadership is not a common construct of everyday life. There lies the problem. To understand what leadership is, or can be, you need to understand what leadership is expected to accomplish.

The first quandary in defining leadership is the qualifying of the term itself. Leadership becomes a concept like art. A piece of art may seem magnificent to some, and mundane to others. Did the evaluator of the art piece understand the artist's goal for the effort? Was the goal of the artist simply to create beauty, or was it the desire to present a

condition of the human experience in visual form? Perhaps both? Did the art piece accomplish the goals of the artist?

This phenomenon is replicated when we attempt to define leadership. As an example, in the next chapter, you will become acquainted with a scholarly book on leadership. It is a marvelous book, full of very well-cited information on all aspects of leadership. However, please note this book's definition of the concept of leadership:

> *"Leadership is a formal or informal contextually rooted and goal-influencing process that occurs between a leader and a follower, groups of followers, or institutions. The science of leadership is the systematic study of this process and its outcomes, as well as how this process depends on the leader's traits and behaviors, observer inferences about the leader's characteristics, and observer attributions made regarding the outcomes of the entity led."* (Antonakis & Day, 2018, p. 5).

Wow! In case you were not counting, this 68-word definition is excellent, academically. But as far as practical, well, not so much. How can a leadership practitioner interpret and then use this definition in everyday leadership centric operations? Although this definition was derived for academic study and use, a precise short and contextual definition is required for practical use. Thus, the reason for this book. This brings us to the practical understanding of leadership.

The best way to understand leadership is to understand what leadership is expected to accomplish. Based on the stated goal of the activity, we can relate the use of leadership by what action is required to meet the expected goal.

Recall that one of the purposes of this book is to simplify a viable definition of leadership. This, in turn, can be applied to known leadership styles or leadership related concepts. A usable definition of leadership should assert the effectiveness of the enterprise. This will lead to a cause-effect relationship between leadership and the desired outcome. In doing so, any or every leadership style can be measured in contrast with this definition.

It is safe to assume there is no 100% foolproof answer to the stated question, i.e. what is leadership? This is due to the complexity of all the applications and expectations of the concept of leadership. In addition, there are exceptions to all practical rules. This is also true for the concept of leadership. However, if we can approximate a definition, and are able to apply this definition to the common leadership concepts, then a starting point and anchor can be used to measure most leadership ideas. In turn, this definition can be applied, in a practical way, to the daily use of leadership. This is one of the main purposes of this book.

Leadership, a new construct.

To define leadership, it is necessary, to begin with, some definite parameters of expectations. Using Isaac Newton's First law of motion, Newton stated: *an immobile mass tends to stay immobile, while a mass in motion tends to remain in motion*. If this law is transposed into the flow of a leadership construct, then we can propose the Input-Process-Output (IPO) model of change.

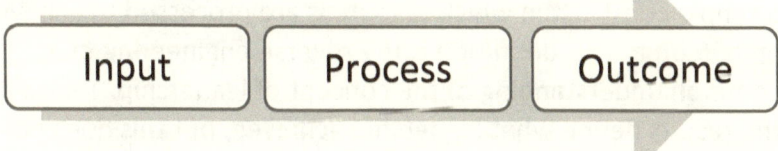

| Input | Process | Outcome |

This model mirrors Newton's First law of motion. Mass is the input, the motion (or lack thereof) in the process, and

the output is the relation between motionless or motion infused action and the original state. So, a definition of leadership can be of similar construct: the input is the resources to be led, the action is the construct in which change is effected, and the output is the desired result.

Therefore, like the I-P-O model of cause-effect, a basic understanding of leadership begins with three items that work together. The first item is the resources to which leadership will be applied as an ingredient of change. The second is the action which creates the impetus for change. The third is the outcome of the combination of resources and actions to achieve the stated goal. Thus, in the most basic form, leadership looks like this:

I-P-O Before:

Input	Process	Outcome

Leadership I-P-O, basic:

Resources	Process	Outcome

This book argues the concept of leadership begins with a simple construct in which resources are processed to achieve an outcome. This definition is the reverse engineering of a common understanding of the concept of leadership. Typically, the results define what leadership achieved, but this does not explain the process. When leadership is usually discussed, the outcome is normally highlighted. In other words, what was accomplished is somehow related to the concept of leadership.

14

Practical Leadership: Making the Case for Synergy

One common explanation of how success was achieved is the "great leadership" applied. However, this is not a definition of leadership per se. A true definition of leadership must explain in its simplest terms (and in concise delivery) what the stated goal was (expected outcome) and the method of attainment (action needed). It is at this point we begin to dissect the resource (input), process and output components of the definition of leadership. We will begin with resources.

Resources. The key objective of leadership involves human activities. Therefore, humans are both a resource to be led and the recipient of the leadership action. The purpose of leadership is to benefit some aspect of the human experience. Leadership is NOT for the exclusive benefit of the designated, or actual leaders. Leadership is a benefit for the team as a whole, with team members and the stated goals being the primary beneficiaries. Any benefit garnered by the leaders is a positive consequence of the accomplishment of the team led as a whole.

By far, the most important resource for a leadership construct is the human element. In fact, you cannot apply leadership tenets to things. Leadership applies exclusively to humans. You may manage or use systems, non-human assets, and peripheral processes. But you lead people. Some would make the case an animal trainer leads a pack of animals. This is true. You could also argue the outcome of animal training involves the betterment of the human experience. This is also true. The difference is the control of the animal is unilateral to the trainer, the animal must comply or be discarded from the activity. The animal does not, per se, choose a leadership construct. The instinct to survive centers an animal's team behavior decision process. Humans, under the true understanding of a leadership construct, can choose

15

compliance with the leadership model used. Thus, we lead people; not machines or systems or animals.

Team members, or resources, are the first component of leadership. Leadership is dependent on the results of the team members. At the very least, leadership involves two individuals. In business or government endeavors, it may involve millions of individuals. No matters how many or how few, leadership needs humans to be a viable construct.

In Chapter 3, the management versus leadership discussion will be addressed. However, it is necessary to address other resources which although not led, are part of the leadership agenda. These resources are managed.

The first managed resource is non-human living entities, such as the aforementioned, animals. Animals will follow an alpha component. This alpha component is a pseudo leader. As mentioned earlier, this relationship is based on the instinct to survive. To survive, a group of animals may subjugate to the directions of an alpha female or male. The betterment of the group is achieved by cooperation. These behaviors do mirror leadership constructs. However, the task related to animal behaviors is related to survival, food and water procurement, procreation, and shelter. If all these needs are achieved, no other leadership quest is realized. Humans demand these needs, and much, much more. This book addresses the hierarchy of more complex needs in humans. It is in this hierarchy of needs where leadership truly flourishes as a concept.

Another resource that needs to be discussed is real assets. Everything from a pencil to complex machines is needed in the construct of successful leadership. These resources are a subsidiary need for the benefit of the intended goal but cannot be led. A machine or real assets does not care. They are only a collateral part of the human experience.

16

Additionally, leaders interact with other commonly understood resources of artificial intelligence or informational technologies. These resources are key to the daily existence of the human experience. As important as they are, they are also not led. Computers are known to interact, quite assertively, with humans. But these devices are not led. They will perform intricate tasks, but only as far as they are programmed. Even if artificial intelligence should approximate acute complex processing capabilities, they can eventually be turned off, re-programmed or destroyed with no moral deficiency on the part of humans.

In leadership, there are interactions between many resources. But the only true resource to be led is the human component. Thus, we now turn our attention to the interaction between the resources (team members) and the leaders. This is the process used to accomplish leadership.

Process. The construct of leadership assumes a deliberate action. Leadership is not a happenstance occurrence. In its most common form, the leader (or leaders) exercise actions to provide the desired team result. In leadership, the actions are deliberate, with intent and purpose. It is possible to have examples where leaders accomplish goals despite themselves. The best analogy of this phenomenon would be a protagonist in a situation comedy show, where they achieve the impossible despite their inadequate mental or physical acuity. In this case, it is either chance or a non-designated leader exercising the leadership construct. To put it in another way, if a leader cannot explain how success was achieved, the leader was at the right place at the right time or an ad hoc leader was the real exerciser of the leadership actions.

It is important to remember; leadership is a human phenomenon. As discussed in earlier paragraphs, there are some leadership attributes in pack animals. There are alpha females or males in pack animals. These individuals exercise control over the pack's day to day activities and control the survival of the pack by hunting, protecting the members against predators, and mating. Nature does give the alpha individual the instinct to assert actions for the survival of the pack.

Humans codify leadership not by instinct, but by intellectual analysis of the effort required to achieve a specific goal. This effort normally does not involve just life's survival. Depending on what team achievements are expected, leadership can bring some type of betterment for the team, and on a grander scale, the community or the human experience itself. For example, leadership in the application of medical research is not just for the positive achievement expectations of the research facility. The effort may provide better medical outcomes to the attenuation or elimination of diseases for all humans.

Furthermore, profit-minded business models try to apply leadership to bring better economic outcomes to the shared holders or owners of the enterprise. In the military, leadership not only looks to accomplish the desired objective, but it also seeks to preserve the lives of the participants in an extremely hazardous environment. Thus, the application of leadership, in general, is an exercise for a better outcome than the original status quo. The outcome is where the center of the leadership dilemma is located. This brings our discussion of leadership towards its relation to the desired outcome.

Outcome. The outcome expected for any organic leadership style is a solution to an issue or issues. This solution is to be a better outcome than the one accomplished by the lack of proper leadership, or any leadership at all. In other

words, any human collective interaction must be benefited by leadership, or the leadership style was incorrectly applied or was non-compatible with the desired outcome. This is one reason why there are definable types of leadership, and these are studied extensively by professionals in academia as well as commercial and governmental agencies. When trying to define a process to achieve an outcome, leadership exposes a complex set of parameters. These parameters require some deliberate interaction to achieve the desired outcome. This is where leadership becomes more difficult to define. There is a complex set of actions and parameters processed to affect an outcome. To use a practical leadership construct, these actions and parameters need to be understood. In addition, this process needs to be simple to understand and simple to apply. So, in order to discuss the term leadership, a more condensed and malleable definition of required actions is needed.

Therefore, one fundamental construct of this book is to be simple in nature. This book seeks to define leadership in a fundamental and simple form, so the construct can be understood by all parties involved. Furthermore, the definition must be able to be applied to most leadership models (or type) and produce measurable data to assert its' (leadership) effectiveness.

Here it comes! With these parameters in mind (Resources, Process, Outcome), we now take the original leadership construct and substitute the three original terms: Resources, Process, and Outcome. As you may recall, earlier we discussed the logical progression of the concept of leadership with a simple schematic.

Adjusted (after 1st step) Leadership I-P-O:

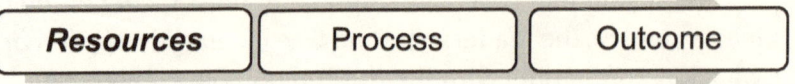

| **Resources** | Process | Outcome |

Now, let's substitute the three elements to codify what we are trying to achieve with leadership. The resources to be led are people, generically understood as humans. Therefore, the word "Resources" is substituted with the word "Human."

Step 1, From:

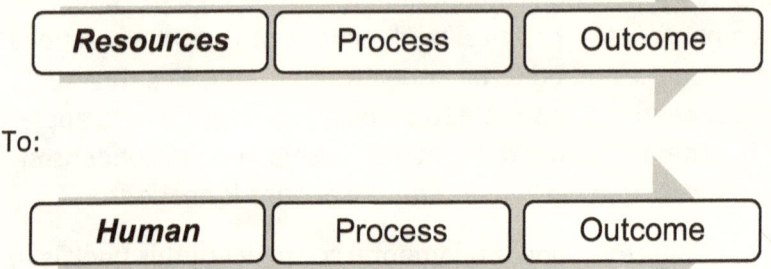

| **Resources** | Process | Outcome |

To:

| **Human** | Process | Outcome |

Next, we need to change the word "process". If the betterment of the group which is led is the desired outcome, then some actions need to be exercised by the group of humans. These actions, or processes, need to be qualified. Therefore, we will change the word "process" with the word "applied". This is done because it is understood there is a direct correlation between the outcome and the input. The interchange between humans and the desired outcome is applied. The word "process" is now changed for the word "applied". Believe or not, we are almost there!

Step 2, from:

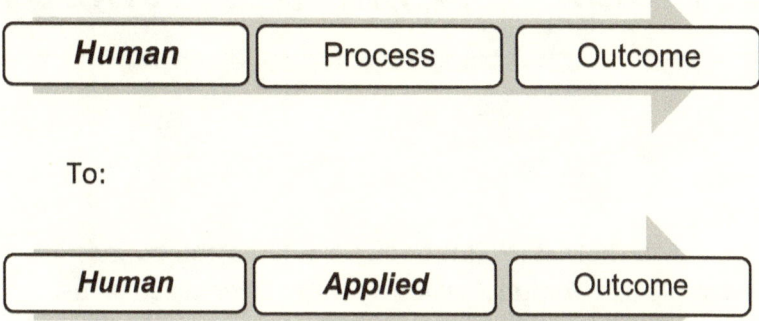

To:

Ideally, the last ingredient for the practical definition of leadership would be one word that explains a better outcome by a group. This desired outcome would be an improvement better than the achievement by individuals of the group, or the status quo. This word would connect the human resources, via an application, to the desired outcome.

Fortunately for us, there is such a word. It is called synergy. There are many ways to define synergy. For the purpose of this book, let's agree synergy is defined as "the aggregate measure of a cooperative effort will be better than the individual efforts in aggregate. (More on this will be presented later, in the discussion of the definition). So, the definition advocated in this book is completed by substituting the word "outcome" with the word "synergy".

Step 3, from:

To, and drum roll please...,

Human | Applied | Synergy

And there it is! This book postulates and defines leadership as *"**Human Applied Synergy**"*. For practical use purposes, the term Synergetic Leadership can and will be used synonymously to explain or use the definition of Human Applied Synergy.

Discussion. The substitution of "human" for the word "resource" is easy to understand. Leadership is not a concept which applies, at least in this book's construct, to anything else but humans. Whether you postulate the human/animal interaction as a possible quasi-leadership environment, the bottom line is most of the leadership centric interactions are within the human experience. Machines, assets, systems and other peripherals of the human experience may be managed but are not led. Leadership is designed to improve the human condition. Any other benefit is part of the dynamic or becomes a collateral benefit.

The word "process" is substituted with the word "applied". This implies action from the leader. As stated earlier, leadership doesn't occur by happenstance. Leadership is a deliberate action, by a leader or leaders. Some leaders are so competent in leadership actions, that the application of the leadership action may seem seamless. This may be true, but the action was still deliberate. The deliberate action leads to the common goal of leadership, which is synergy.

Thus, the word "synergy" substitutes the word "outcome". Synergy is like explaining offsides in a soccer game. It is hard to explain in simple terms, but to an avid fan (or referee, or coach, or player), it is easy to see. In simple terms, synergy presents the benefit of cooperation. As mentioned earlier, synergy is generally understood as: The collaborated (cooperative) aggregate score is better than the individual scores combined. As an example, supposed a 10-question algebra test was given to 10 random individuals, of different ages and walks of life. These individuals cannot discuss or copy the answer from another participant. After the test is concluded, the scores are added for a total score.

Then you take the same individuals, give them a similar test, but in this instance, they can collaborate to find the correct answers. When you compared the results of both sets of tests, the cooperative aggregate score (2nd test) will be better than the first effort. The difference in scores is the result of cooperation and sharing of knowledge. This cooperative effort improved the test scores for every one. Even if one individual understood all test questions, she or he could raise the entire group score. Let that sink in for a minute.

Thus, a leader who applies synergy with other team members, or a group, will accomplish a better result, than just simply instructing all individuals to perform a task(s) separately. In a synergetic leadership environment, a leader seeks synergy to produce the best possible outcome for the stated goals.

Another benefit, "closing the loop". Both the Input-Process-Model and its leadership derivative, Human-Applied-Synergy, follow a simple linear flow. This is short-sighted. There is more, much more. True leadership "closes the loop." This is to say the synergetic process starts and ends at the same place.

23

In the case of synergetic leadership, the "loop" begins and ends with the human resource.

Again, borrowing from our understanding of a different discipline, communications, synergy follows a known construct. Synergetic Leadership follows what we understand as the communication loop. In the communication loop, a sender sends a message which is received by the recipient. At a minimum, the recipient sends a reply message to verify the receipt of the sender's message. This is the way communication should work.

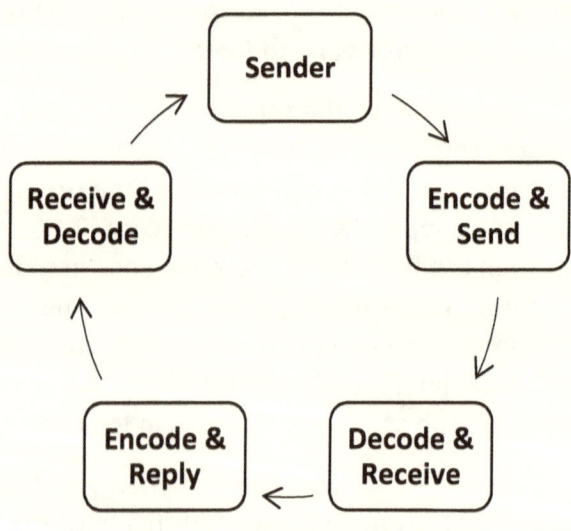

The Synergetic Leadership model should work somewhat similarly. The closing of the loop should also benefit the team in general.

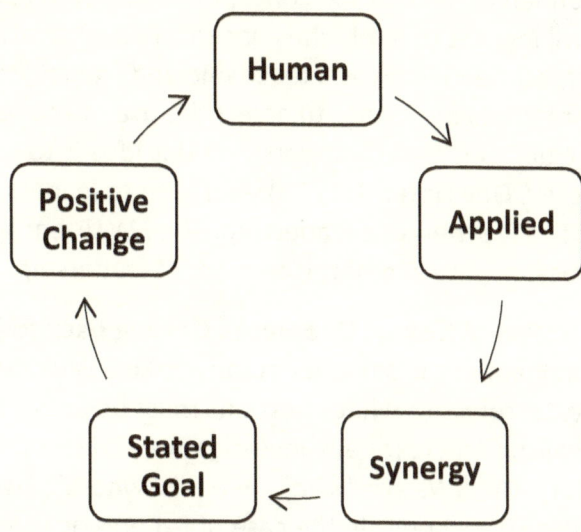

This means achieving the stated goal should lead to the benefit of the team, and not exclusively the leader(s) or stated goal. When a goal is stated, synergy does not only deliver the stated goal. The use of synergy will result, achieve a positive change for the team. This is accomplished in many ways. For one, synergy allows for all members of the team to cooperate towards the stated goal. Based on my military experience, this leads to pride of ownership of the solution. This is because the cooperation was the instrument of achievement, so each team member was part of the success. Secondly, synergy allows the passing of knowledge and/or experiences between team members, which allows the sharing of team strengths and the knowledge and attenuation of the team's weaknesses.

The key component of this loop is the leader's understanding of the concept of synergy, and the willingness of the leader to apply the concept successfully. Chapter 3 discusses the attributes of a synergetic focused leader. Although different personalities can enhance or diminish the synergetic attributes of leadership, it is not necessary to have a specific temperament to be a synergetic leader. All it takes is the understanding of the concept of synergy in leadership, and the willingness to apply the concept. The application of synergetic leadership is a teachable and trainable construct. It only requires the leader to assert the use of this leadership construct. One way to understand this idea is to use the "Five Whiskey, One Hotel" (5W1H) approach to leadership, and specifically synergetic leadership. The 5W1H encapsulates the practical application of the concept of leadership.

Five Whiskey, One Hotel. Getting back to journalism? The alphanumeric alphabet acronym, Five Whiskey, One Hotel or 5W1H refers to what questions must be answered by a good journalistic article (or any investigative endeavor, for that matter). The 5Ws are "who", "what", "where", "when", "why", and the 1H is "how". In the case of Synergetic Leadership, it is prudent to discuss the 5W1H model.

In Synergetic Leadership, the "who" applies to all actors, the leadership cadre (leader) and the follower cadre (team). The leaders provide the format and impetus for the goal to be achieved. The followers cooperate in the effort, by providing replies and input toward the stated goals. The "what" is very simple. "What" is the reason for the use of a leadership construct, i.e. the team stated goals. The desired result is the reason a leadership scheme was used in the first place. So, the answer to "what" becomes the team's goal.

The next two questions are open-ended, and as a definition or construct, are of minimal importance. "Where" and "when" can be easily explained by asserting the place and time where the leadership construct is applied. Although the result may be specific to a place (where) and has specific constraints of the time allocated (when), these two terms are most generically applied to the common concepts of leadership. Thus, Synergetic Leadership does not need a specific time and place for its' applicability. This is also true to other leadership concepts.

The "why" is the reason for the study and use of leadership concepts. This book makes a case for the need for synergy to efficiently and accurately execute the team goals. Note that this sentence is also true to other leadership constructs. In just about any group challenges, leadership is the force multiplier toward achieving team goals.

This leaves the "how" of the inquiry. In the case of Synergetic Leadership, the "how" is the leader's ability to use cooperative efforts of the team to produce the desired result. Otherwise, the desired result could not be achieved or may have been achieved with significant deficiencies. The best leadership outcome can be produced using synergy. Can this axiom be as easy as it sounds? Well, no, there is a "catch".

There is always a catch. It is hard to conceptualize a perfect leadership construct, especially if a construct is conceived as a practical endeavor. This is true for the case of Synergetic Leadership. In the practical application, Synergetic Leadership can be negatively affected by some type of counter-team endogenesis. The practical application of Synergetic Leadership reflects the outcome of synergy, in other words, a better outcome is derived by team cooperation. Can this cooperation be foiled? Yes, unfortunately, it can.

In the example provided earlier, with the 10-question algebra test, synergy could have been spoiled. For example, one of the team members could have known one or all the correct answers, and either not share the knowledge, or worse yet, knowingly gave the wrong answers. Is this part of the practical application of leadership, especially a synergetic model? No, it is not.

27

This is where the importance of the word "applied" comes front and center. There may be members of the team which behave in a way to mitigate team success or produce stated goal failure. These individuals are counter-team actors. If a counter-team actor tries to sabotage the synergy required for success, then this model is not synergetic. The practical use of leadership is now crippled. The leader must correct this issue immediately. The key to regaining the synergetic advantage is to correct the behavior, not correct (or try to) correct the person(s). Therefore, the leader must neutralize the counter-team actors' behaviors to counter the degradation (or loss) of synergy.

The counter-team behavior may be a partisan issue or anti-symbiotic, self-centered behavior of known or unknown origins. Furthermore, the behavior may be temporary, or fully continuously engaged. These individuals must be removed from the synergetic caucus until the behavior can be redirected towards a synergetic approach. This may include dismissal. In either case, it is the behavior, which is addressed and not the individual per se. This issue will be discussed in more detail in Chapter 5.

It is sufficed to understand a synergetic model of leadership expects and/or assumes the synergy construct is understood by all team participants, (including and foremostly the leader). This is not to say team members need to like the attempted goal or the participation of other team members. The leader must accept the responsibility to focus the synergetic effort on the stated goal. The stated goal should be the measure of success. The personal interactivity component can and should be, addressed at the appropriate time expeditiously. Otherwise, synergy may degrade all the way to failure. The key point is synergy, as a minimum, should operate as a form of "détente." The concept is to work together, even if we would rather be with a different group. A competent

synergetic leader will accomplish the task of extracting synergy regardless of any human interactive deficiencies.

A practical way to think about the issue of counter-team actions can be surmised as follows. Do the right thing, at the right time and for the right reason. The right thing is the application of synergy, even if the counter-team actor chides away from the stated goal. If synergy cannot be achieved with the counter-team member(s), dismiss these actor(s) from the team. If the dismissal of counter-team actors is not an option, then try to deviate or lower the counter-team influence to the lowest point possible. The right time is when synergy is required to complete the stated goal. In other words, when the goal requires synergy (and in leadership it does), apply the concept continually, and with maximum effort.

The right reason is the stated goal. This construct should give a method to attenuate or avoid counter-team actors. Finally, one more issue: what if the leader has partisanship or egocentric issues himself? In this case, a review of the stated goal from team members is required. If the stated team (leader asserted) goal is counter to the organizational goals and expectations, then the discrepancy must be addressed with the leader. If such an exchange is not fruitful, consideration to address this issue to a higher echelon authority is required. It is important to remember the main impetus of Synergetic Leadership is the stated goal and not the leader per se. This issue is further discussed in Chapter 5.

Summary. A common, granular and concise definition of the term leadership does not exist in the academic world due to the complexity of the term "leadership." Leaders would benefit if such a definition could be found. The concept of synergy offers a plausible and workable definition of leadership. Synergy thus allows a practical application of the

29

concept of leadership. The Synergetic Leadership model makes the case to use group effort to accomplish a stated goal by having the team members cooperate with their individuals' strengths. This effort simultaneously counters or attenuates the team's weaknesses. The focus is on the stated goal. The leader uses all available resources to enhance synergetic outcomes. The concept of Synergetic Leadership is not academically proven, but based on known construct and experience, it is palatable to assert its usefulness as a leadership style or model. Absent proof to the contrary, Synergetic Leadership provides a stable construct to develop other modes of applicability.

Synergetic Leadership is not a perfect construct. The main variable is the personal predispositions or biases of the led individuals. The leader may have these issues also, but the leader is not the center for synergy. The stated goal is the center impetus of the synergetic actions. The leader's behavior can be addressed by consult or higher echelon engagement. To attenuate these variables, counter-teams behaviors need to be identified and engaged in the desire for a synergetic environment.

Chapter 2, Reader Beware!

The next chapter, Chapter 2, is mostly academic (read boring) and painfully lengthy. It encompasses 82 pages and approximately 19,600 words. This chapter was written to give the term Synergetic Leadership contextual academic validity. If you are searching for synergetic application and therefore not interested in academic discourse, bypass Chapter 2. If you are reading this book with an academic interest, read this next chapter last. If you are suffering from insomnia, read ahead. It may provide relief for the sleeplessness!

Chapter 2

Synergetic Applications of Leadership Concepts

"She blinded me with science!" Song, Thomas Dolby

Science and other academic disciplines struggle with the concept of leadership, both in the definition and applicability. Yet, any concept of leadership is only as useful as its' relative applicability with other known leadership terms. In other words, where does our concept of Synergetic Leadership stand in relationship among known leadership constructs? Making a case for Synergetic Leadership requires this leadership style to be conceptually compared, contrasted, enhanced or disputed against a myriad of other useful leadership concepts.

In this chapter, a set of commonly understood leadership terms will be presented. These, in turn, will be individually compared to the term Synergetic Leadership. It is not intended for this book to advocate any specific leadership style, to include Synergetic Leadership. The comparison is only meant to contrast In general terms. This is done so you can interpret the case presented for Synergetic Leadership and derive your own conclusions. The benefit expected of this

31

chapter is to think of leadership centrally and comparatively, wherever the journey should take you.

The terms presented in this chapter were extracted from an academic book, *The Nature of Leadership*, by John Antonakis and David V. Day (Third edition, 2018). This academic book is used in a Doctorate of Strategic Leadership program curriculum. The terms of this book will be explained in its basic form. This is done in the interest of practicability of use. This practicability will be compared to the term Synergetic Leadership to make contextual comparisons between terms.

The methodology of the presentations will be in 4 categories: Definition, Comparison, Contrast with Synergetic Leadership and Conclusion. For abbreviating purposes, each term presented will have the following 4 named sub-sections: **Definition, Comparison, Contrast,** and **Conclusion**. The terms are presented in alphabetical order.

1. *Authentic (Ethical) Leadership.* M. Gandhi

Definition. An Authentic Leadership model is founded on the intrinsic human attributes of the leader. It is also known as Ethical Leadership. These attributes and leadership style are exemplified by the work of Mahatma Gandhi. Gandhi was a social activist who pursued peaceful civil disobedience to help achieve India's independence over British rule. His emphasis was always a human desire for freedom, and he accomplished his goals with perseverance against large odds. His leadership style was truly authentic.

An authentic leadership style attempts to match a humanistic or altruistic focus of the leader with the success of the team. This leadership style defines leadership as a positive process, where the emphasis on the leader's moral and humanistic approach leads to the achievement of the stated goals. In essence, the leader facilitates a team environment for success, based on team concentric social attitudes. This style of leadership mirrors other newer leader styles to be discussed later.

Authentic leadership is at its core, both the desired process and a desirable outcome. This desire is positive but is constrained by the moral foundation of the leader (Antonakis & Day, 2018, p. 68). For the purposes of this book, the assumption begins with the idea of this leadership construct, and the authenticity of the concept is for the greater good. For both leaders and followers, leadership must be a real and desirable outcome of the effort applied. But to advocate an Authentic Leadership model, a definition of the word "Authentic" needs to be understood.

If the term authentic means real, or true, to who is the realness or trueness directed? Is the authentic model directed to describe the relationship between followers and leaders? Or does the term authentic become the determinable factor in the process of leadership? Or is it a hybrid? Thus, Authentic Leadership is easily valued as a leadership style, but difficult to pinpoint as a process.

Comparison. In the Authentic Leadership model, the focus is centered on the leader's humanistic attributes. This is to say the leader has certain positive social interactive skills that translate into a cooperative environment. The environment is centered on the leader's interpersonal skills. These interpersonal attributes are the key to the team's success towards the stated organizational goals.

The leader will probably use some type of social exchange to achieve success. Synergy may be one of many tools the authentic leader uses. It is possible the authentic leader can use multiple leadership styles and attributes to achieve the stated goal. These could include charisma, team-centered communication or personal interactive skills. Yet, no matter what inherent skill set the authentic leader brings to bear, the fulcrum of Authentic Leadership is centered on the leader and the leader's processes, and not on the results achieved by the synergy.

Contrast. The Authentic Leadership model centers the idea on the leader attributes as delivering or enhancing the effort required to reach the stated goals. On the other hand, synergy focuses on the process of how leadership is achieved. In Synergetic Leadership, the focus is on the cooperative effort of the team members. Authentic leadership is leader centric. Synergetic Leadership is a process and outcome centered. The outcome of Authentic Leadership is derived from the attributes of the leader. In Synergetic Leadership, the outcome derived is by synergy, with the process as the center of success.

In Authentic Leadership, a "great leader" is required for success. In Synergetic Leadership, success is achieved by the process and the willingness of all participants to engage in the challenge and solution. In Synergetic Leadership, a "great" leader is not required. The most important factor is to understand and apply the concept of synergy.

Conclusion. It is easy to agree, or advocate for, a leadership model to be authentic. Authentic is a word with positive synonyms and understood as a desirable trait. Authentic Leadership appears to be an altruistic centered style. However, Authentic Leadership seems to describe the "what" of the 5W1H model, and may even explain "why", but not necessarily "how". Synergetic Leadership explains how, that is to say, synergy is a collaborative effort. This collaboration achieves a better outcome than otherwise could be achieved by the same amount of resources (team members).

2. *Authoritarian Leadership.* Drill Sergeant

Definition. The authoritarian style of leadership is perhaps the easiest to perceive. This quintessential model is a leadership style used by training non-commissioned officers (NCOs). At basic training in the military, or in cadet training in military officer preparatory schools, this leadership style is categorized by top-down, direct issuance of instructions (orders) by the designated leader. Immediate and complete compliance by team members is expected, and for the most part, demanded.

Recall, as you will, the basic inquiry of this book in Chapter 1, i.e.? *"Why do they yell so much?"*. It may appear to the untrained eye (or ears) to be an unnecessary imposition to the receiver of the yelling. But under the tough, acerbic and neo-toxic social exchanges between the authoritarian leader and team members lies a very good reason for the harsh treatment. There are various reasons for the use of an authoritarian style of leadership. The first one is group and individual discipline.

When correctly used, Authoritarian Leadership seeks group and individual team member cohesiveness towards the stated goals. The instructions (orders) given are expected to focus the entire team on what the leader (or the stated goals) are determined to achieve. No variations of compliance or time constraints are allowed because there is no available variance of actions or the time allowed towards the stated goal.

In the case of timing, the correct use of the time allotted in military operations is a key to success. The precision of a target engagement with the right type of assets at the right time is necessary at all times. Therefore, team members in a correctly applied Authoritarian Leadership style are required to act when and where they are needed with no hesitation or misunderstanding.

Furthermore, the tasks required for success must be accomplished as planned, precisely. Think about a direct infantry attack to an enemy's position. The team members must understand precisely what is immediately expected and act accordingly with precision. This is achieved so the attack can react to possible enemy's counteractions. Enemy's actions are an ever-changing dynamic of a possible attack.

Authoritarian Leadership is also used when the leader(s) have complete control of data, processes (or both) towards the stated goals. In order words, the team members are only engaged to the extent of tasks needed to complete the stated goals expected by the Authoritarian Leader. These are not necessarily military, or para-military operations. This method of authoritarian style of leadership can also apply to highly sensitive environments such as operating a ship, directing air traffic control, firefighting, or police officer engaging an active shooter.

The whole idea is to exert artificial overwhelming authority to complete the stated goals. In other words, in the absence of evidence for contrary action, the directives of the authoritarian leader must be accomplished. This action is in the best interest of both the team and the desired results. In this environment, the validity and usefulness of Authoritarian Leadership are necessary. However, if Authoritarian Leadership is used at any other time, demagogy and oppression occur. Neither demagogy nor oppression is recognized as an attribute of proper leadership.

Comparison. Both synergetic and authoritative styles of leadership seek cohesive group accomplishment of the stated goals. In Authoritarian Leadership style, the center of gravity is the designated leader. In its basic form, the authoritarian leader holds and understand the data and processes required for task completion. The responsibility and accountability of the stated goals reside primarily, and sometimes exclusively, on the leader. This latter observation leads us to contrast synergy and the Authoritative Leadership style.

Contrast. Because Authoritative Leadership amounts to leader centric leadership, an often-revealing attribute is the rigidity of the use of authority. Authoritarian leaders tend to be rigid in the approach to the leadership exerted. This is counter-indicated to the synergetic model. This book will explore this deficiency in Chapters 4 and 8.

It is more common to understand and like synergetic styles of leadership because synergy assumes all team members have a positive influence on the stated goals. This influence is proprietary to the individual team member. This contribution is also possible in an Authoritative Leadership environment, but only to the extent the authoritative leader encourages or allows to be used. The bottom line is the authoritative leader is the center of the direction of the team.

Conclusion. Although generally perceived in a negative "light", there is certainly a place for Authoritative Leadership in the "team toward stated goals" spectrum of leadership styles. Military, paramilitary, sports teams and others have used, and continue to use, an authoritative style of leadership. Most of these examples provide a case for the use of Authoritative Leadership to produce desired stated goals. The misuse, or worse yet, abuse of such construct can be devastating to the applicable team. However, other leadership styles may be misused or abused in a similar way. Therefore, Authoritarian Leadership is an appropriate leadership style when such an approach toward the stated goals is required.

3. *Charismatic Leadership.* Frederick Douglass

Definition. As opposed to the Authoritarian Leadership model, one of the most appealing models of leadership is the Charismatic Leadership style. In terms of charisma and eloquence to lead a cause, history regards Mr. Frederick Douglass in the highest esteem. Mr. Douglass was an abolitionist who tirelessly advocated the abolition of slavery prior to and during the American Civil war. His excellent charisma was demonstrated in his oratory, and his writing as well.

Like Mr. Douglass, a charismatic leader influences the team by making the team identify with this type of leader. In this construct, the charismatic leader imparts a sense of equitability with team members. This process motivates the team towards the completion of the stated goals. The engine behind the success of the stated goals is the devotion of the team toward the charismatic leader. The interpersonal skills the charismatic leader portrays has a multiplier effect on team members. For example, research has found that charismatic leaders "increase followers' self-worth through emphasizing the relationship between efforts and important values" (Antonakis & Day, 2018, p. 65). Therefore, Charismatic Leadership can be used to extract better performance from a team, compared to the status quo.

Comparison. It is easy to understand the charismatic leader shares some attributes and constructs of Authoritarian Leadership. In Authoritarian Leadership, the direction or orders are obeyed regardless of the team member likeability of the designated leader. In Charismatic Leadership, the team identifies with the excellent motivational skills of the leader. Although there is a difference in the social exchange between Authoritarian and Charismatic leadership styles, both leadership styles are essentially leader centric styles. Synergy may be expected or could be developed, but it is not a central impetus toward the achievement of the stated goals.

Contrast. When compared to Synergy, or Synergetic Leadership, Charismatic Leadership shares some common attributes. Mostly, the ability to use interpersonal skills with team members is noted and shared by both Synergetic and Charismatic Leadership styles. However, the contrast is on who is the center of the impetus towards the effort. In Charismatic

39

Leadership, the center of impetus is the designated leader. In Synergetic leadership, the impetus is on the team members and the team member's efforts toward the accomplishment of the stated goals.

A "darker" side of Charismatic Leadership is the possible development of zealotry. There is no perfect leadership style or leader, regardless of which leadership environment is present. Therefore, when the team's followership is motivated by a charismatic leader to follow a path that is illegal or immoral, then the attributes used under the purview of Charismatic Leadership are nothing else but a form of demagogy.

Conclusion. In isolation, charismatic leaders instill a sense of team identity with the leader to motivate the team members towards the stated goals. If a charismatic leader, in addition to individual exceptional motivating skills, uses the synergy of the team members toward the stated goals, then the combination of both charisma and synergy should produce excellent results. In a synergetic model of leadership, cooperative skills are the stated important attribute for success.

4. *Collective Leadership.* Lord of the Flies

Definition. As the name implies, a collective leadership environment is one in which the leadership roles are shared by the team members. In this leadership style, "leadership is broadly distributed among a set of individuals instead of centralized in hands of a single individual who acts in the role of a superior" (Antonakis & Day, 2018, p. 43). It is very similar to the holder of the conch scenarios in the book *Lord of the Flies* (W. Golding, 1954). In this Nobel Prized book, (1954), whoever held the conch (during group gatherings) held the authority to speak. In the gatherings, the conch was passed around to signify the team member's turn to speak. The conch symbolized temporary authority. Likewise, in a Collective Leadership environment, the temporary designated leader holds the responsibility and accountability for the delivery of the stated goals. The leadership responsibility and accountability of the stated goals are shared in turns.

Comparison. The concept of shared effort is quite synergetic. In Collective Leadership, the synergetic effort is the share of responsibilities and accountabilities of the temporary leader with team members. Each current leader may provide a different approach to the challenges of the stated goals from previous (or future) temporary leaders. Each temporary leader provides the best leadership efforts based on this individual's best leadership attributes commensurate to the stated goals. There is an opportunity for multiple ideas. Since no two leaders are identical, there is a synergetic effect of every temporary leader giving their "best take" on the challenges presented. Subsequent leaders may emulate the effort, improving the delivery of the stated goals. This cooperative effort is a synergetic mode of delivering leadership constructs.

Contrast. The strength of Collective Leadership can turn into a liability. It is very difficult to centralize goals when each temporary leader finds a different way to deliver stated goals. There could be a tendency to follow a very specific aspect of a stated goal at the expense of others. As an example, an accounting centered temporary leader may hold financial goals

41

to higher importance than an engineering centered temporary leader. As a temporary leader, the latter may hold systems development a higher priority than financial priorities. So, when conflicting impetus from temporary leaders occur, then the overall leader of the team (team **non-temporary** leader) may have to redirect the direction of the team.

Conclusion. There is synergy in Collective Leadership. But there are also significant challenges in using a model of Collective Leadership. There has to be a relatively stable amount of resources among temporary leaders to benefit from Collective Leadership. Although it is understood Collective Leadership provides an impetus of new ideas by subsequent temporary leaders, time constraints and changes of the stated goals may limit the Collective Leadership synergetic gains. When these constraints appear, the current temporary collective leader may not be the best suited for the change in priorities.

Furthermore, the amount of time a temporary leader has must match the abilities of the designated temporary leader attributes and the scope of the stated goals. These times "at the helm" have to match the results of previous and future temporary leaders. Mismatch in time or scope of leadership may be contraindicated to the synergetic health of the team.

5. *Contingency Leadership.* Emergency Room

Definition. The term Contingency Leadership relates to the leadership is exercised when there is a reactive or constantly changing environment. This style describes "leader-member relations, task structure and the power of the leader determine the effectiveness of the type of leadership exercised" (Antonakis & Day, 2018, p. 10). The reactive environment may be issues of resources (team members, time, equipment) or stated goal (the outcome has changed). For example, a contingency can occur when the delivery of stated goals in a specific situation and the timing of the events exceeds the available resources. Let's use the Emergency Room (ER) scenario. The ER may be equipped to provide critical care to several patients, depending on the number of personnel or logistics assets (beds, operating rooms, etc.). Suppose there be a school bus highway accident, with over 75 casualties. A contingency situation now occurs. The staff is more than willing to provide the needed services (stated goals), but this particular ER is deficient in the number of assets it can bring to bear (beds, operating rooms). Note that it is not a lack of desire of the team, it is simply too many casualties with too little space.

Even if the medical facility were able to accommodate the immediate arrival of 75 casualties, then time may become a performance disruptor. Time is the other condition of a Contingency Leadership scenario. With the immediate requirement of delivery of the stated goals (emergency critical care) to 75 patients nearly simultaneously, the amount of medical expertise may prove lacking.

Medical facilities have contingency plans for these scenarios. However, a leadership style has to match the situation. The determinant of this scenario is the situation, not the leader itself (Antokanis & Day, 2018, p. 140). Thus, Leaders must adapt to the situation presented. The leader's traits and behaviors become an important factor in the delivery of the stated goals. Of the desired traits required for successful employment of Contingency Leadership, adaptability is key. Leaders performing in a Contingency Leadership situation must adapt to the environment immediately and deliver the stated goals. To use a common colloquialism, Contingency Leadership seeks to "make lemonade out of lemons".

Comparison. Synergy and adaptability can be symbiotic. Synergy is a protocol to find solutions to a problem. Likewise, adaptability is the ability to react to different situations. Synergy is adaptable. In fact, the reason to use synergy is to adopt a better solution using a cooperative effort. Competency of a leader using synergy to resolve unforeseen or unusual situations should produce a better result than the leader going "solo" with the solution. This adaptability to use synergy in a contingency situation, (as opposed to whatever leadership style was currently used), can be a key factor in resolving the current contingency.

Contrast. As a basic construct, synergy (or Synergetic Leadership) is group cooperation dependent. Contingency leaders are adaptability and competency dependent. In the ER case mentioned, the ER leaders must understand and be competent in the delivery of the necessary actions to save or preserve lives. It is natural to assume contingency leaders will benefit from synergy to solve problems. However, the time constraints in contingency situations are more in line to have competency take primary importance over synergy. This primary importance occurs during the contingency. At other times, contingency leaders will benefit from synergetic input towards the stated goals of the next expected or possible contingency.

Conclusion. The key elements for a leader in a Contingency Leadership scenario are adaptability to the situation at hand and the adaptability use of resources to solve the dilemma presented by the contingency. In contingency situations, success is measured by the delivery of the stated goals regardless of the difficulties encountered by the contingency. Leaders are selected to deliver success. A contingency leader does so by competence, adaptability, and when possible, synergy.

6. *Entrepreneurial Leadership.* Steve Jobs

Definition. Entrepreneurial leadership is obviously related to the concept of entrepreneurs and entrepreneurship. Antokanis and Day state: "The notion of opportunity is central to most contemporary definitions of entrepreneurship" (2018, p. 386). It doesn't take much convincing Steve Jobs, the founder of Apple software and computers, was an entrepreneurial leader. Not only did Mr. Jobs lead the development of software and hardware systems, but his devices have also changed the way the entire world interacts. Mr. Jobs was the creative impetus for the company he envisioned.

Entrepreneurs are a part of the creative aspect of the human experience. The way these individuals contribute relates to the effective and creative use of ideas. Entrepreneurship seeks to find new ideas to address old or emerging issues. It is a creative venue to solve problems. In

45

terms of leadership, the same approach is used to extract a team benefit toward the stated goals. Entrepreneurial Leadership leverages creative new ideas to achieve the stated goals.

One of the aspects of Entrepreneurial Leadership is an inherent tendency for a paradigm shift. This means these leaders are not immune to shift the processes or focuses related to the achievement of the stated goals. If the current paradigm is not producing the stated goals, then the entrepreneurial leader will set in motion a new set of resources or employ the existing resources and processes differently.

These types of leaders also are well in tune with seeking new opportunities. New opportunities may exist in the current construct of the operation, or in new constructs not used before. The idea is to seek a new answer to an old question or to seek a new idea to new challenges. Either way, entrepreneurial leaders are looking, metaphorically, for "a better mousetrap."

Comparison. Entrepreneurs, or leaders practicing Entrepreneurial Leadership, seek a new or better solution. By definition, synergy should provide better results. In this case, a better solution can be achieved by synergy. Therefore, it is easy to state Entrepreneurial Leadership goes "hand in hand" with Synergetic Leadership. The two concepts are compatible and symbiotic. An entrepreneurial leader can seek the "better idea" and give a low value to whom or how the solution is reached. Normally, the entrepreneurial leader applies synergy. However, the case can be quite different.

Contrast. The overlap between Synergetic and Entrepreneurial Leaderships may not happen due to the limited attributes of the leader. It is entirely possible to be a great entrepreneur and lack the skills to apply synergy to solve challenges towards stated goals.

For example, there may be a lack of charisma or interpersonal skills on the entrepreneurial leader. Although eager to search for new ideas or seek new opportunities, if a leader cannot exert a desire for a group to achieve the entrepreneurial activities, then the entrepreneurial leader becomes deficient in exploiting this leadership style.

In such a case, the entrepreneurial leader may have to engage in other leadership styles to achieve the application and execution of new ideas or opportunities. It is also possible to perhaps engage in a form of Shared Leadership. In this case, the entrepreneurial leader concentrates on the development of new ideas or opportunities, and a shared leader concentrates on the use of such ideas with the assembled team. Shared Leadership will be addressed later in this chapter.

Conclusion. It is not too difficult to recognize the world is full of visionaries with the idea of "building a better mousetrap". Those who can develop these new ideas or find new opportunities will benefit from the results of such better ideas or opportunities. As a leadership style, entrepreneurship does present a prospect of achieving new or better-stated goals. Entrepreneurial leaders benefit greatly by using synergy, since the core idea may be improved (or a paradigm shifted) with the application of a cooperative group effort. However, it is in the purview of the leader to communicate and process the synergy required to succeed as an entrepreneur. A different leadership construct may need to be applied. This may include some form of Shared Leadership. Otherwise, the entrepreneur may have to accomplish the stated goals alone. The latter is not a practice of leadership. An ad hoc leader may provide a balance between entrepreneurship and leadership. The entrepreneur could focus on the ideas and the ad hoc leader could focus on the team's involvement.

7. *Exploitive Leadership.* Saddam Hussein

Definition. Unfortunately, it is very possible you have experienced, (or know someone who has experienced) an Exploitive Leadership environment. This leadership style is characterized by some, or perhaps all, deficiencies of human attributes.

Exploitive Leadership employs direct or indirect manipulation of the team for the achievement of the stated goals. The detriment of the team, either physical or mental is of little or no concern to the leader. Exploitive Leadership is Machiavellian, i.e. the end justifies the means. It is to "win at all cost", including the human cost. Research has concluded Exploitive Leadership can yield benefits (Antonakis & Day, 2018, p. 45). However, this leadership style is toxic to the human experience and counter-indicated for long term success in the environment which it is used.

A contemporary example of this leadership style is Saddam Hussein. This president of Iraq ascended to power and led Iraq with an exploitative leadership style. He coerced the Iraqis to follow his priorities with intimidation or violence. He even attempted his exploitative leadership transnationally by invading Kuwait. This last action precipitated the demise of his rule.

As with Saddam Hussein, history remembers many political and social structures that employed Exploitive Leadership. Normally the center of gravity, the exploitive leader, uses all aspects of this leadership style. The termination of the use of Exploitive Leadership involves the separation of the exploitive leader from the exploited teams. Either the leader leaves or is removed. In some cases, the entire team evacuates the environment. In any case, the quicker the exploitive leader leaves the environment, the quicker the normalization of the human experience can return.

Comparison. It is with great trepidation a comparison between Exploitive Leadership and Synergetic Leadership is made. This trepidation is due to the idea that it is possible to force synergy between team members in an Exploitive Leadership environment. An oppressed team member can be coerced to apply Synergetic Leadership with other team members by using fear or oppression as the motivating agent. Such a team member may make the case that if the forced synergy is not achieved, the environment will deteriorate worse than the present condition. In slavery, slaves can be coerced to cooperate with other slaves. This disgusting approach may work. But in order to continually achieve the stated goals by forced synergy, a continued set of team members is required to replace the exhausted team members already exploited. Eventually, this factor, among others, weakens the Exploitive Leadership environmental existence.

Contrast. Exploitive Leadership is the antithesis of Synergetic Leadership. Exploitive Leadership is utterly and completely non-synergetic. In terms of synergy, you may think there is a dichotomy between what is stated in this paragraph above. There is no dichotomy. Recall the stated definition of

49

Synergetic Leadership in this book: **Human** Applied Synergy. The expectation of a humanitarian approach to the concept of leadership is a core value on the stated definition. Simply forcing synergy does not rise to the level of expectation of the human experience. The application of synergy must commensurate to the value of the human experience, i.e. Synergetic Leadership values the team member with at least equitability to the stated goals. In Exploitive Leadership, the only value assigned to humans is the cost of achieving a goal. Notice the use of the term "a cost", and not "the cost." In Exploitive Leadership, especially in its' extreme form, the human value is at par with other resources and nothing else.

Conclusion. With all the understandings of the human experience, it is hard to fathom the desire to use Exploitative Leadership. This leadership style goes against any humanistic applicable constructs. Unfortunately, it is continuously used in environments across the globe. Whatever gains towards a stated goal are reached using exploitation, the price paid at the expense of team members does not justify its use.

8. *External Leadership Environment.* The FAA

Definition. As the name implies, the external leadership environment is the scope of resources and processes that reside outside the direct control or direct influence of the led enclave. It is important to understand the External Leadership Environment can induce controls or influences on the leadership used towards the organizational stated goals. The reverse is also true. The leadership enclave can induce changes to External Leadership Environments. (This condition will be discussed later in the Internal Leadership Environment section). These mutual and continuous environments work with, or against each other, in the practical application of leadership.

To understand how the External Leadership Environment influences control on an organizational leadership construct, look no further than governmental regulatory compliance. A leader may try to instill ideas or solutions to stated goals which are not permitted by law or governmental regulations. For example, freight delivery systems (whether airborne, rail or over roads) are regulated to ensure a level of safety for both the deliverer of freight and/or the general population. No matter if the regulation creates a burden to an organizational leadership priority, the compliance is still mandatory. In this case, the external leadership environment constrains the leadership enclave to the degree which protects the interest of the community in general.

There are cases where the opposite is also true. A prime example would be leadership in companies which design, and sell unmanned airborne systems (UAS), or drones. The Federal Aviation Administration (FAA) has always had regulatory control over aerospace vehicles. But with the availability and exponential use of UAS devices, the FAA had to adopt old and create new regulations to protect other users of the aerospace environment from drone usage. In a way, the mere development of the drones and their increased use precipitated a change of regulatory compliance. The leadership enclave (drone manufacturers) influenced changes to the External Leadership Environment (the FAA).

Comparison. As stated previously, there are direct and indirect controls and influences bearing between the External Leadership Environment and the opposite, the Internal Leadership Environment. (As mentioned earlier, the latter will be discussed further in this chapter). The External Leadership Environment attempts to deliver policies and processes with the understanding these dynamics may influence some changes to the affected organizations. It is understood under a leadership construct, the influence or control exercised by the External Leadership Environment is meant to benefit the External Leadership Environment primarily. However, this benefit can also extend to the leadership enclave affected by the control or influence of the External Leadership Environment.

If synergy is used between the leadership and external leadership environments, the solutions and approaches may result in an acceptable compromise between the interest of both parties. Therefore, synergy may provide a conduit to allow external leadership environments to benefit the leadership enclave affected, and vice versa.

Contrast. There may be friction between the leadership enclave (internal leadership environment) and the External Leadership Environment. This friction may not be intentional, but it is problematic just the same. The synergy between the External Leadership Environment and the affected leadership enclave can result in a better outcome, rather than the status quo. If synergy and cooperation are not attempted or are deficient in scope, then the External Leadership Environment may produce a detrimental challenge to the leadership enclave affected.

Conclusion. The External Leadership Environment affects the organization which receives influence or control of such processes. Sometimes the control or influence works the relationship in reverse. The friction caused by unwanted control or influence can be attenuated or improved using synergy. The cooperative effort between the External Leadership Environment and the leadership enclave should provide an agreeable solution to the challenges presented by the relationship.

9. *Inspirational Leadership.* Lee Iacocca

Definition. Similar to the charismatic leader, an inspirational leader makes the case for the achievement of stated goals by having the team identify with the purpose of the stated goals. The main difference between the two is the interpersonal interactive style used. Recall the charismatic leader centers the stated goal achievement with the team identifying with the leader. The inspirational leader uses personal influence to codify the team members' understanding of the challenge presented.

A good example of an Inspirational Leader is Lee Iacocca's work with automobile development and sales at Chrysler Corporation. In the late 1970s, Chrysler was failing at developing and selling its automotive products. Mr. Iacocca was hired and in a short time turned the company around. He mastered the ability to inspire confidence in the products he developed and sold, to both the employees who were manufacturing them and the consumers who were buying.

As Mr. Iacocca did, the inspirational leader alludes to the need for extra effort or sacrifice to achieve the stated goals. The actions required by the team are of higher moral importance. This, in turn, motivates the team for a better effort towards the stated goals.

Comparison. When compared to Synergetic Leadership, it is easy to see the compatibility with Inspirational Leadership. The inspirational leader makes a case for the synergetic sacrifice of the team to achieve the stated goals. The ideas developed by the team are important to achieve the stated goals. In addition, the effort to achieve such stated goals follows a sacrificial effort for attainment. Both Synergetic and Inspirational Leadership try to emphasize the benefit of the stated goal compared to the effort required. The way this comparison is achieved is by indicating the higher moral, ethical or altruistic value of the stated goal commensurate with the team's effort. The team focuses on what amount of effort is required. However, the effort is of secondary importance when compared to the achievement of the state goals.

Contrast. Inspirational leadership does not have to be charismatic, or synergetic either. In contrast with the charismatic leader, an inspirational leader does not seek or need the led team in identifying themselves with the persona of the inspirational leader. In Inspirational Leadership, it is the stated goal that centers the team's priority, not the leader's inspirational style of achieving such goals. The center of gravity in Inspirational Leadership is the ability of the leader to communicate a sense of "we can do better" toward the stated goal. It is of little importance if the team identifies with this leader. The primary importance of the team is to focus on the altruistic value of the stated goal. The led team accepts the committed effort toward the stated goals as the means to achieve an improved result.

54

Interestingly, an Inspirational Leadership style may accomplish the stated goals and not be completely synergetic. Some team members value moral, ethical, or altruistic goals differently. Therefore, there may be team members who will comply with the effort required to attain the stated goal for a multitude of other reasons not related to the Inspirational Leadership itself. In other words, some team members will cooperate with inspired team members to achieve the stated goal, but not be inspired by the inspirational leader. In this case, synergy is achieved. This is to say a cooperative effort to achieve the stated goals is exercised. However, the effort required by these team members was not centered on the leader's inspirational style of leadership. The effort may be derived by the individual team member's desire to accomplish an altruistic goal individually, with synergy or inspirational leadership an ancillary input.

Conclusion. Inspirational Leadership creates an environment where the leader persuades goal achievement by having the team members assert efforts under the construct of a "we can do better." This "we can do better" is a sacrificial priority higher than the team members themselves. The motivation of the team members is derived by the sense the effort expended has significant value. The value of the stated goal mirrors this "higher calling" value. This is to say, the moral, ethical, or altruistic reason for the stated goal inspires the team towards the stated goals.

10. *Instrumental Leadership.* Military Logistics

Definition. Instrumental Leadership is a bit of a misnomer. To understand this concept better is to perhaps call it "conduit" leadership. In this style of leadership, the leader centralizes the leader-to-team member construct by providing resources for the team members. So, the leader is primarily "instrumental" in providing the resources for stated goal achievement.

Attributed to Napoleon Bonaparte, French General, and Emperor is the axiom in the military that states "An army travels on its' stomach". This means no food, no army. As great as a general can be in strategy and tactics, if the general cannot provide food for the troops, the campaign will fail. One main reason for Robert E. Lee surrendering his Confederate Army (at Appomattox Courthouse) was he had ammunition to fight, but his army lacked in food. What Napoleon Bonaparte and Robert E. Lee were referring to was resources toward the stated goals. These resources facilitate the effort required to achieve the stated goals. For example, suppose a software team is creating a new set of programs to start (or enhance) a new application of a business model. An instrumental leader may help the team by modifying the work schedules, providing a separate area to brainstorm ideas, or allow non-standard use of work time to enhance creativity, etc. Therefore, the instrumental leader is acting as a facilitator, or a conduit to have the designated teams achieve the stated goal.

The instrumental leader may be part of the team itself. In the case above, the instrumental leader may be the lead programmer. However, the context of this style of leadership speaks to what the leader is doing to facilitate, or improve, the environment needed for the achievement of the stated goals.

However, an instrumental leader may not be directly "hands-on" with the team either. There may be a gap in the leadership hierarchy between the beneficiaries of Instrumental Leadership and the instrumental leader himself. A case of this is the strategic aspect of Instrumental Leadership.

Human Resource Managers may, in fact, be instrumental leaders. These professionals deal with pay issues, the company provided insurances and other benefits. Without the existence and provision of the actual assets (salary and benefits), and the processes to provide these resources employees, i.e. team members, it is doubtful any stated goal would be achieved. In the case above, the Human Resource Manager may not directly be aware of the coming and goings of the software development department. Yet, without the delivery of the salaries, benefits and other human-centered resources, the assembled team may not be able, or even willing, to achieve the stated goals.

Comparison. In Instrumental Leadership, synergy may be consequential to the provided actions of the instrumental leader. In other words, synergy is achieved by the instrumental leader addressing the processes and interactions which make the team members operate better as a whole. In such a case, Synergetic Leadership is achieved in subterfuge. The instrumental leader provision of processes and other resources results in better synergy between team members. The instrumental leader fosters synergy by providing the resources to create or amplify the synergy between team members. Yet, the instrumental leader may be using synergy as a means to an end. This "means to an end" is the contrast between Instrumental Leadership (means) and Synergetic Leadership (cooperative effort).

Contrast. In Synergetic Leadership, it is the application of synergy which represent the primary construct toward the stated goals. In Instrumental Leadership, the primary construct is the process to provide resources to create or enhance the synergetic environment. These two elements, working towards the completion of stated goals do not have to be or are desired to react, as a mutually exclusive paradigm. It is easy to see the symbiotic nature of both Instrumental and Synergetic Leadership working together.

Synergetic Leadership uses any and all resources to ensure synergy is optimized for the achievement of the stated goals. Instrumental Leadership provides a process-to-team conduit to enhance the ability of the team to achieve the stated goals. Both leadership style helps the other simultaneously. Without the resources and process required for success, synergy is degraded. Without synergy, the instrumental resources and processes bear little value toward the stated goals. Therefore, both Synergetic Leadership and Instrumental Leadership coincide with the purpose of achieving the stated goal but differ on how the leadership is accomplished. Synergetic Leadership is a cooperative approach. Instrumental Leadership is a resource centered approach.

Conclusion. Instrumental Leadership acts in a logistical spectrum of attainment of the stated goal. The influence of Instrumental Leadership is related to the resources and processes required by team members to accomplish the desired tasks toward the stated goals. The input provided by an instrumental leader may be synergetic. However, the synergetic aspect of an instrumental leader's actions may be of indirect consequential effect. The instrumental leader's main concern is to provide the resources and processes to achieve the stated goals. The synergy achieved by this action is complementary to the intent of the instrumental leader.

11. *Intergroup Leadership.* Air Traffic Control

Definition. In basic terms, Intergroup Leadership refers to the interactions and relationships between different groups, as they collectively attempt to achieve a stated goal, or goals (Antonakis & Day, 2018, p. 312). Any leadership enclave will have challenges related to the inner workings of the group led. This happens every day, at every hour, at Air Traffic Control centers (ATC) worldwide. The path of an airplane is directed and tracked by an air traffic controller. Since ATC is divided into sector areas, these professionals must coordinate with each other on the altitude, speed, and direction of every aircraft airborne. Failure of deconflicting would result in catastrophe i.e., aircraft collision.

The challenge presented by air traffic control is an Intergroup Leadership issue. Normally, the challenges of any leadership enclave are human, process, and resource-related, or a combination of the mentioned. However, in Intergroup Leadership these resources are contained in the purview of the members of one group trying to achieve the stated goals for the larger organization, i.e., air traffic control.

Thus, in Intergroup Leadership there is a crucial distinction. The synergy required is now embracing different groups simultaneously. This is a crucial aspect of Intergroup

Leadership. The challenge posed by Intergroup Leadership is the cooperation requirements between multiple groups working together synergistically toward overall stated goals. To achieve synergy across different groups is very complex. This complexity stresses the required cohesion of a synergetic environment.

Comparison. Intergroup Leadership seeks the exact same result as Synergetic Synergy. This is to say the intergroup leadership relation seeks to achieve the stated goal by intergroup cooperation, which should involve synergy.

Depending on the dynamics of the stated goals, each group (i.e. different ATC sectors) provides a different set of inputs or results to accomplish the overall stated goals. This aggregate cooperation is very synergetic. The mere fact a set of groups (or leadership enclaves) are required to cooperate speaks volumes on the need for synergy. Inside these groups, there is a synergetic expectation of cooperation between the group members to produce the group's contribution to the overall stated goals.

In aggregate, the contributions of all the "sub-groups" should provide a synergetic answer to the challenges presented by the overall stated goals. But the practice of leadership is not that simple. There are issues of friction between the cohesiveness inside the individual sub-groups, and the cohesiveness between these sub-groups in the collective effort. This brings the dilemma to the issue of identity.

Contrast. Groups tend to create and believe in their own identity. This identity may serve well inside a group (or sub-group) and produce a synergetic effect of cooperation and compliance inside this group. By common arithmetic, it could be assumed the more synergy applied to the overall stated goal (by sub-group aggregated efforts) the more synergy is derived. In Chapter 6, an anomaly of this approach will be discussed. The bottom line is the possibility of increased synergy by the plurality of groups (in this case sub-groups) could produce more synergy towards better overall stated goals. Yet, this may not be true. More does not necessarily mean better. This may be due to the difference in the relationship between the hierarchal enclave leadership and the subordinate (subgroup) leadership team members. Because sub-groups identify themselves more with their particular leadership (sub-group) relationship, there can be a disconnect between the perceived overall goal (hierarchal) and the sub-group goal.

To achieve overall synergy, or at least deter erosion of the synergetic results, the overall leader (or leaders) must simultaneously address two notions. The first is to accept and acknowledge the variety of sub-groups required to achieve the overall stated goals. By doing so formally, the identity of the sub-groups and the relationship between the sub-group leader and their respective teams are not threatened.

Secondly, the overall leaders need to recognize the fact there will be an asymmetry of perceived (or actual) efforts and recognition of the sub-groups' synergetic involvement. This asymmetry is a discrepancy created by the overall stated goal and is not reflective of the desire or abilities of the subgroups. In other words, there may be an asymmetrical effort or comparative result by sub-groups. Yet, there is synergetic cooperation required by all sub-groups for the success and attainment of the overall stated goals.

61

Conclusion. Intergroup Leadership is related to leadership enclaves cooperating to produce overall stated goal(s). The overall goal affects all sub-groups directly or indirectly, and the cooperative effort of all group members is required for the accomplishment of the overall stated goals. There is a frictional aspect of intergroup cooperative dynamics which intergroup leaders must address. The main reason for this friction is the tendency for sub-groups to identify themselves organically at the expense of the overall group. Intergroup leaders address this dilemma by recognizing this phenomenon and motivating overall cooperation (synergy) to achieve the stated goals.

12. *Internal Leadership Environment*. FAA

Definition. As it can be obviously deducted, Internal Leadership Environment refers to the scope of influence within a leadership construct or enclave. This environment is characterized by the ability of the leader to exert influence on team members. Because of the size, and normally, the proximity of the leader to the team, actions may seem to happen quicker. These actions also seem to affect more directly the team members as a group, or as individual members. Note the Internal Leadership Environment does not necessarily mean the team is under one roof, or even near in actual proximity to each other. With the advancements of technology, a virtual office can create a synergy of many individuals who are hundreds, if not thousands of miles away. So, it is not the physical closeness that creates an Internal Leadership Environment. The internal aspect of this environment is created by the relationship paradigms between leadership and team members. The closeness is the construct of the direct leader to team member exchanges. Normally, the External Leadership Environment reacts to the actions of the Internal Leadership Environment. This is because the Internal Leadership Environment normally acts as an impetus to the External Leadership Environment.

However, the relationship between both can be reversed. The input or task created by the External Leadership Environment may produce changes to the tasked agency. Recall the example used in the External Leadership Environment section, the Unmanned Aircraft Systems, or drones.

In this example, the Federal Aviation Administration, or FAA, begins to regulate the use and applicability of drones. This would seem to be a corollary application to manage the airspace occupied by both drones and manned aircraft is functional. However, in reality, this regulatory control exercised by the FAA is actually a reaction to the development and increased proliferation of the use of drones. In this example, an Internal Environmental Leadership enclave, the designers and developers of drones, created a situation where an External Leadership Environment had to react. This regulatory reaction was to protect the safety of the airspace between manned and unmanned aircraft. This reaction by the FAA is a response to the development and proliferation of UAS.

Comparison. A practitioner of leadership should easily understand the comparison between an Internal Leadership Environment and the External Leadership

Environments that influence the former. Leaders should understand the need to synergistically solve issues created by either. Both environments seek a beneficial result toward their respective stated goals.

In reality, both environments are seeking comparatively the same results. Both environments strive to solve the challenges presented to them by the other. Where the challenge originates may be different, but the desire and focus are very similar in delivery. Both environments should work synergistically with each other.

Synergy could be used, or certainly should be used, by both parties to achieve the stated goal of each environment. In both the internal and external realms of leadership, the mere word "environment" implies multiple groups of individuals, systems, and processes. In synergetic leadership, these groups cooperate to achieve the stated goals. Therefore, whether the issue is evoked by the internal or external environments, leaders should work synergistically to achieve the stated goal of both entities.

Contrast. The contrast of the two relates to the scope of influence and the perceived hierarchy. In the External Leadership Environment, the scope is usually outward from the organization (as the title implies). These outward systems influence the organization. Normally, this influence is originated by outside forces, and the organization must react to these inputs.

In reaction to the challenge presented by external environments, leaders in the internal leadership environments react to address whatever external issues are at hand. The results of these reactions are forwarded from the Internal

Leadership Environment outwardly toward the external environment for resolution.

External Leadership Environments are perceived to have the above hierarchy over the Internal Leadership Environments. This perception is of little value. In synergetic Leadership, it is the cooperative effort (how the problem is solved) that is of the highest importance, and not who has primacy. Although it is important to note the relationship between the two distinct spheres of the leadership environments, it is not materially important to distinguish a hierarchy. As presented before, a synergetic leadership construct centers on cooperation, and not on process ownership.

Conclusion. Internal Leadership Environments represent the inner workings of the leadership construct. Normally, this environment refers to leaders and team members addressing the issues presented by external environments. The external environments do present issues for internal environment resolutions. However, the reverse is also true. Products and processes created in the Internal Leadership Environment do exert and influence changes in the External Leadership Environment. The relationship between the two environments tends toward synergy.

13. *Interpersonal Leadership.* *"Widget" Production*

Definition. Interpersonal Leadership is commonly understood as the relationship between the team member and the leader. It follows a simple concept. It is understood the leader and the individual team member exchange real quantitative resources and perceived qualitative sources to achieve the stated goals. This exchange essentially makes the organization successful, even though the exchanges are "one on one" between a leader and each member of the team.

Real resources exchanged between the leader and the team member are easy to understand. For example, monetary incentives are a real and quantitative resource to both participants of the exchange. The team member may be manufacturing or servicing a quantitative measurable item. In this exchange, value is easily understood. The more "widgets" you make, the more salary or benefits the team member may receive. These are easily measurable and clearly understood by both participants of the Interpersonal Leadership relation. However, in some Interpersonal Leadership exchanges, the exchange between the team member and the leader is harder to quantify.

Trust and respect are examples of understood qualitative resources that the team member exchanges with the leader to balance the leader to the member exchange equation. Note that the leader is exchanging something easily measured and receiving a quite different resource. This is not like going to an international bank where dollars may be exchanged into Euros and the balance of the transaction valued by the agreed exchange rate. The leader is exchanging something measured quantitatively (monetary incentive) and the team member is exchanging a qualitatively measured resource (trust or respect).

Yet, these exchanges are valuable and result in improved organizational effectiveness. The key to Interpersonal Leadership is to understand the individuality between the leader and a team member, as opposed to the leader and the team. The team member's value is derived by the identity of the relationship to be on a one-to-one basis with the leader. Team members who participate in an Interpersonal Leadership style identify more with the leader than the group.

The key to success, and simultaneously the challenge of the Interpersonal Leadership environment is the ability of a leader to address the motivational needs of each team member. This must be done while simultaneously centering focus on the team's stated goals. The fact is each team member is an individual, perhaps with unique motivational needs. These members require a leader to perceive, understand and react to the individual team member's respective motivational needs. "Different people have different interests, and it is often not self-evident to individuals that they would prioritize the collective interest over their individual pursuits" (Antonakis & Day, 2018, p. 313).

Comparison. Synergy applies to a one on one basis. The two individuals engaged in an Interpersonal Leadership model meet the minimum participant requirement for synergetic applicability, two individuals. The exchanges between the two participants are designed for the accomplishment or improvement of the group's stated goals. Therefore, Interpersonal Leadership is synergetic in nature. Whether the interpersonal exchange is a static construct (i.e. the algorithmically derived amount of salary versus productivity) or negotiated between participants, the exchange is active between the team member and the leader, and therefore synergetic.

Contrast. Although synergetic, the challenge is for the leader to understand the wide variety of motivating exchanges between each member of the team. The larger the team, the larger this challenge will become. Getting to understand what improves the motivation of each individual team member takes time. This challenge is further exacerbated if there is a high turnover rate among team members.

Conclusion. Interpersonal Leadership leads to interpersonal exchanges between leaders and each individual team member. The leader offers real quantitative resources to motivate team members to improve the accomplishment of the team's stated goals. In return, individual team members give the leader quantitative resources (production goals) or qualitative resources such as trust or respect as them (individual team member) response to the exchange. In many cases, both quantitative and qualitative resources are exchanged. These exchanges are effective and favor the individual team members who identify themselves with the leader. These exchanges are synergetic. The challenge of Interpersonal Leadership is the ability of leaders to understand the individual motivators of each team member. This challenge is due to many factors, of which the size of the team and the turnover rate are noteworthy.

14. *Irresponsible Leadership.* Bernie Madoff

Definition. An irresponsible leader is the result of inappropriate or illegal use of any resources. A classic example is Bernie Madoff, a well-known irresponsible leader. Mr. Madoff was a financial investor who took millions of dollars from investors doing Ponzi schemes. In a Ponzi scheme, existing investors are paid by the investments of new investors. In this case, Irresponsible Leadership was the result of willful illegal transactions of available resources. However, in Irresponsible Leadership, it is not necessarily the intent of the leader to do harm. But leadership is not measured by intent, it is measured by results. Sometimes, even good organizations do the wrong thing for a perceived right reason.

The attributes of leadership are intended to be positive. This book makes a case for synergy, to be understood as a positive use of a leadership construct. Positive outcomes or results are common goals expected when applying leadership concepts. Otherwise, the result is demagogy. Unfortunately, even the positive aspects of leadership can turn into a negative outcome.

Irresponsible Leadership can normally be traced to the rigidity of beliefs or actions (Antonakis & Day, 2018, p. 480). Any organization model itself by the social environment in which it operates. Social expectations change, and organizations that do not change with new discoveries of expectations are prone to react to a new standard irresponsibly.

Manufacturing businesses are a good example of this phenomenon. A manufacturer of a specific item may find no harm in producing and selling a specific type of product. It may

69

be legal to do so, and the manufacturer accepts and manufactures the product following all regulatory restrictions.

Unfortunately, 10 years later, it is found the product can produce some type of harm to its' users. Yet, there is no regulatory change to support this new finding. The manufacturer continues to produce and sell the product under the auspices there is nothing illegal with either the manufacturing or selling of the product. This may be true, but society now instills a moral dimension to the exchange between the manufacturer and the consumer. Ignorance or compliance of regulatory standards no longer shields the moral responsibility of the manufacturer. The manufacturer is practicing Irresponsible Leadership.

Why? Because the accountability of leadership is based on the best (read highest altruistic value) outcome for **both** the manufacturer and the consumer. Thus, shareholders of the manufacturing company are not the only affected entity. The entire society affected is a form of a shareholder of the company.

Organizations that operate and react with the best interest of the relationship of both its shareholders and the social environment will tend to act responsibly. Organizations that hold steadfast rigidity to known principles tend to, by default, allow irresponsible leadership actions.

Obviously, if the organization purposely acts in an irresponsible matter, then the accountability for these actions is easy to judge. In such a case, irresponsibility may be, and often is, an unethical or criminal action. These actions are outside the norm of a leadership term. This is because leadership's goal is to benefit, and not harm the society served at large.

Comparison. To do no good, cooperation may be required. If an attempt to engage cooperation with leadership, (albeit irresponsibly), is being considered, then there is some type of cooperative effort. This may mirror a synergetic construct because the effort is cooperative amid the irresponsible leaders and team members within the organization. Yet this contrasts with the true definition and purpose of Synergetic Leadership.

Contrast. Cooperative efforts are normally required to accomplish Irresponsible Leadership. As mentioned previously, these cooperative efforts have a synergistic component. But Irresponsible Leadership lacks the human benefit component. This case is made in this book's definition of Synergetic Leadership. The component missing is the benefit to all involved humans. Whether purposely or casually, the mere fact there is a lack of an improvement of the human condition makes Irresponsible Leadership part of the opposite spectrum of the synergetic leadership construct.

Conclusion. Irresponsible Leadership is an anomaly of the leadership spectrum. It can be in response to rigidity or steadfastness of a previously understood paradigm. However, paradigms do change due to societal changes. The changes modify the accountability of organizational processes and products. Lack of adaptation of such changes can produce irresponsible outcomes to previously known acceptable leadership actions. Although irresponsible actions can have a cooperative component, these are not synergetic per se. This is because it lacks a human beneficial component required for Irresponsible Leadership to be synergetic.

15. *Laissez-Faire Leadership*. *"Hands-off Boss"*

Definition. The concept of Laissez-Faire involves the idea of autonomous team members being left alone in pursuit of whatever is being attempted (as an organization). In Laissez-Faire Leadership, the leader is concerned with the application of this autonomous construct. However, this generally means "a failure to take responsibility for managing" (Antonakis & Day, 2018, p. 250). A good example of this leadership style would be a leader who is mostly absent from the role of leadership because of incompetence, or undesired to lead. The common idiom for this type of leader is to be "hands-off". This does not imply the leader keeps his distance from the team members. This does mean there is relatively less interaction between leaders and team members than normally expected from other leadership environments.

Laissez-Faire Leadership may be useful in some situations. First, in specific stated goals, autonomous thinking may be required. In an organization where creativity is a vital part of goal achievements, some team members will be more creative when working autonomously. For example, an advertisement creator may spend hours alone trying to develop a new ad campaign. In this case, this individual may work alone.

Another way Laissez-Faire works is if the interaction of the team member requires very individualized focused work. Think of a computer technician or a chemical researcher. In these cases, the team member is focused on actions that require intensive and singularly directed attention. These professionals are left alone to pursue their required tasks.

In either case, there are specific reasons a leader may be "hands-off". When these reasons are task-related, there is a benefit for the team to accomplish the desired tasks toward the stated goals. However, there is one mode where Laissez-Faire is contraindicated as a leadership style.

As mentioned earlier, there are other reasons the leader does not engage with the team. A leader may not know the need for leader-to-team engagement requirements (ignorance). The leader may not want to engage due to a lack of interpersonal skills (does not know how). Or the leader does not actively want to engage with the team (active engagement rejection). In any of these cases, the Laissez-Faire environment is not healthy. The leader may also not be able to engage because of absenteeism from the group. In this case, the autonomous nature of the team members' effort is temporary. To abate leadership absenteeism, a temporary leader can be assigned until the permanent leader returns.

No matter the reason for a leader not wanting to engage with the team, this Laissez-Faire environment may not be conducive to success. If so, this anomaly must be addressed by the team, or the leader's peers, or the leader's hierarchy. Laissez-Faire style of leadership is only appropriate where specifically needed. Laissez-Faire Leadership is contraindicated in any other situation.

Comparison. Laissez-Faire Leadership can be synergetic. The application of synergy is not necessarily a constant, day-to-day engagement. Synergy is used when needed. There is no extra credit for continuous synergetic engagements unless these engagements are necessary. In some leadership environments, autonomous actions are required to achieve the stated goals.

Contrast. Laissez-Faire Leadership can tend to make people disengage with team members, and slowly erode the advantages of a synergetic environment. Laissez-Faire tends to benefit introversion and may be contraindicated for heavily extroverted team members. Also, note the leader must clearly understand the process for the achievement of the stated goals. This, in turn, may require an unusual number of autonomous tasks from team members. In such a case, the Laissez-Faire leader may benefit from the complete understanding of how the organization operates, and what is required from the leader to operate efficiently and progressively with autonomous team members.

Conclusion. At first glance, Laissez-Faire Leadership appears to be operating with a leadership style detached and distant from the team members. This may not be true. Laissez-Faire Leadership is appropriate when low levels of direct interaction are expected, or the task specificity of actions requires autonomy to be successful. Laissez-Faire is not appropriate when it is the leader who detaches himself from the team members. Such detachment is detrimental to team cohesiveness and/or stated goals accomplishments.

16. *Mutual Leadership*. Joint Military Operations

Definition. Mutual Leadership equates to peer leadership (Antonakis & Day, 2018, p. 173). The easiest way to understand the concept is to understand leadership laterally. Mutual Leadership is the action among multiple leaders to enhance or assert the accomplishment of stated goals. This leadership construct takes advantage of the knowledge and experience of various leaders interacting to solve the challenges represented in each leader's separate led sections, or the common organization as well.

Think of Mutual Leadership through the actions of a Military Joint Operation. The specific skills and assets of different branches of service come together for a common goal. Navy assets may be bombarding a target, while Air Force airplanes provide air cover over the battle area. All this could be happening as Marine and Army infantry units deploy to engage the enemy near the bombed target. The commanders (leaders) of the units engaged interact laterally with each other to achieve the mission objectives.

The relationship of mutual leaders may be similar to the leader to team member exchange. There may be exchanges of ideas and processes which by comparison present a better solution. The difference between Mutual Leadership and other forms of leadership is Mutual Leadership exchanges are mostly lateral or are expected to be lateral. The interactions are with colleagues. In other forms of leadership, the exchanges are vertical in nature, as the leader relates to the actions of subordinates or the team members.

It is important to note Mutual Leadership does not need to be inter-organizational. It is common for leaders of an organization to meet and discuss departmental resources and processes. These discussions may produce a more desirable result directly related to the organizational stated goals. In these cases, the interaction is organizationally based, centered on the desired goals of the organization.

However, Mutual Leadership can be practiced externally. This can happen when leaders benefit from collaborations of other leaders outside the organizational sphere. In this case, a leader can provide perspective to the leadership issues to a different colleague. An example of this would be Mutual Leadership discussion among technically centered organizations. The venue could be a professional symposium. A leader may have an issue and look for colleague assistance in the resolution of the challenge.

Comparison. Mutual Leadership is obviously very synergistic. There is an understood benefit in the cooperation between peers in leadership environments. The effort among peers or colleagues helping each other should produce a better solution than if the leaders attempted success by themselves. Thus, the same construct of cooperation between leaders and team members apply equally when the cooperation is lateral. Synergetic gains are a natural outcome of Mutual Leadership.

Contrast. Since the comparison between Mutual Leadership and Synergetic Leadership shows strong affinity, there is very little to contrast. There are differences between the two concepts, but they are not of substance. The only perceptible contrast is the center of impetus. As described earlier, Mutual Leadership tends heavily on a lateral dimension. This is to say mutual leaders are providing synergy among themselves. Synergetic Leadership tends to have a vertical dimension. The exchange is mostly between the leaders and the team members.

Conclusion. Mutual Leadership is a synergetic, beneficial activity between leaders. The relationship is lateral among the practitioners and can be beneficial intra-organizational. Mutual Leadership can be practiced outside the confines of an organization as a colleague derived exchange of ideas applicable to multiple institutions. Mutual Leadership follows the tenants of Synergetic Leadership. The only minor difference is the lateral nature of Mutual Leadership when compared to the vertical nature of Synergetic Leadership.

17. *Neo-Charismatic Leadership.* Tele-Evangelists

Definition. Neo-Charismatic leadership is, as the title implies, a new form of delivery of the leadership attributes of the classical charismatic leader. In order to understand Neo-Charismatic Leadership, it is necessary to recall some tenants of Charismatic Leadership itself. The goal of a Charismatic leader is to achieve organizational success by motivating compliance of the team members' task requirements towards the stated goals. Charismatic leaders encourage and motivate to the point where team members identify themselves with the leader. This encouragement is emotionally centered. This produces a sense of the singularity of purpose, and a synergetic delivery of the stated goals.

In Neo-Charismatic Leadership, identity with the leader is also desired. The difference is the way this identification is achieved. The symbolism, emotional delivery and the sense of the singularity of purpose are delivered by a form of infusion. The delivery system may not be as emotionally charged as the classical charismatic leader. The medium may be different. Instead of a congregation of team members for a live presentation, a neo-charismatic leader may make the case for effort in written format or visual aids. In other words, the goal of charisma is the same, but the delivery is different. This style of leadership is common with Tele-evangelists. Using mass media resources, the Tele-evangelists give an emotional and symbolic message to convey the desire for an altruistic goal.

The reason for this change can likely be attributed to how information is dispersed organically through society. Where formerly televised events would require a United States president to assert Charisma and "make the moment count," it is now possible to reach even more people by various information systems such as podcasts, streaming informational systems, web distributional content, etc. Thus, the message delivered may be the same, but the delivery is different.

In addition, the neo-charismatic message may also need to differ somewhat from the charismatic leader. Social changes that tend to require an affinity engagement with a leader can force leaders to adapt the message to the recipients' requirements. The message once delivered with strong verbal exuberance may not receive the same acceptance today. A neo-charismatic leader may find a different way to state a case. The delivery may state a more easily understandable substance (data, expectations) for a specific case. This information then produces a sense of identity of team members with the neo-charismatic leader based on the information, more than the style of delivery.

Comparison. Both Charismatic and Neo-charismatic styles of leadership seek team member synergy. They both strive to have an actual or symbolic identity with the leader. To either leader, this connection is what motivates the team members to produce results in the accomplishment of the stated goals. Therefore, synergy is attempted by the identification of team members with the leader. This team identity leads towards synergy among team members themselves, and among team members and the neo-charismatic leader.

Contrast. In Neo-Charismatic Leadership, as well as the classic charismatic leadership model, the emphasis is on the leader. This does not mean that synergy is not valued. But the value is leader centric derived. Synergetic Leadership makes the case the team members synergetic impetus provides the process to achieve the stated goals. Whereas in either charismatic leadership process, the leader takes center stage to motivate achievements, in Synergetic Leadership the value is placed on the team member synergetic effort.

Conclusion. Both Charismatic Leadership and Neo-Charismatic leadership seek stated goals' achievement by the identification of team members to the applicable leader. This relationship motivates the team member toward the accomplishment of the stated goals. These leadership styles do not contrast against synergy. Either type of charismatic leader seeks a synergetic effort from team members. The main difference is where the value is centered between charismatic leadership and a synergetic leadership model. The charismatic leadership model center the emphasis on the leaders, and these leaders' individual abilities to motivate team members to identify with such a leader. In the synergetic leadership model, the center of emphasis is the team members' effort to accomplish the stated goals.

18. *Organizational Leadership.* Balancing Multiple Environments

Definition. Organizational leadership, as the title implies, is the integration of systems and processes which are part of the operational construct towards the achievement of the stated goals of an enterprise. Depending on the type of organization, the purpose of such an organization dictates the stated goals. The Organizational Leadership cadre then reacts to these stated goals with appropriate team members-to-leadership systems. To accomplish these stated goals, the components of the Organizational Leadership construct need to balance four different environments.

The first environment is team members centric issues. The Organizational Leadership balances the expectations and needs of the team members against the requirement to achieve the stated goals. The design of the team members centric leadership system is usually done as part of the strategic planning of the organization. These include salaries, compensation, and leadership-to-team member relational structures.

The second environment of the organizational Leadership construct is the involvement of capital centered shareholders. These individuals provide the capital required to produce the desired goals of the organization. Organizational Leadership interacts with these individuals by ensuring the capital offered by the shareholders is rewarded, in turn, with some form of profit. The Organizational Leadership construct now balances the addition of the capital shareholders in addition to team members.

The third environment to be balanced by the Organizational Leadership construct is regulatory in nature. The limits by law or regulations apply a counterbalance to both the need to deliver the stated goals and satisfy the needs and expectations of both shareholders and team members.

Finally, the fourth environment of this construct is the relationship with the community at large to the actions of the organization. The Organizational Leadership construct must address the impact of operations in the local, regional and global communities. This relation between the organization and community transcends the legal or regulatory threshold level. The community at large expects an altruistic delivery of the enterprise's stated goals which coincide with the social expectations of such community. The visual representation looks something akin to this diagram.

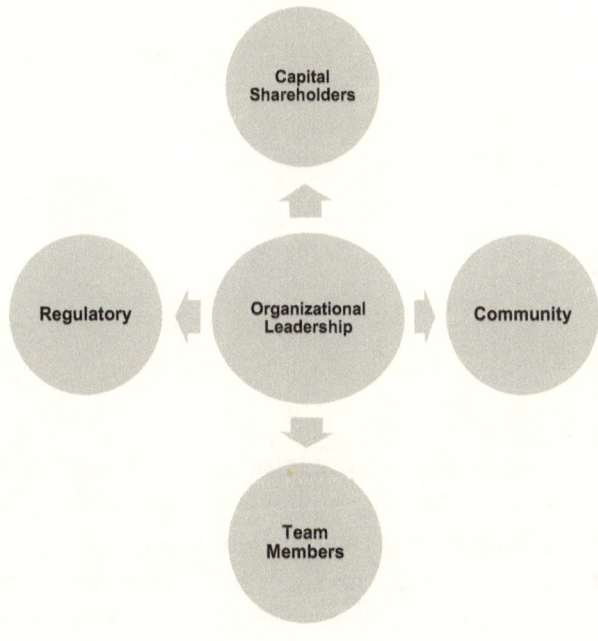

An important aspect to consider is the non-stationary representation of influence or importance of the environments presented. The diagram presented before shows the level of importance between the Organizational Leadership and the 4 environments as both static, and vertical. This is not true. The relation is both vertical and lateral, where any environmental area can assert primary importance at any time due to actions or expectations among the organization.

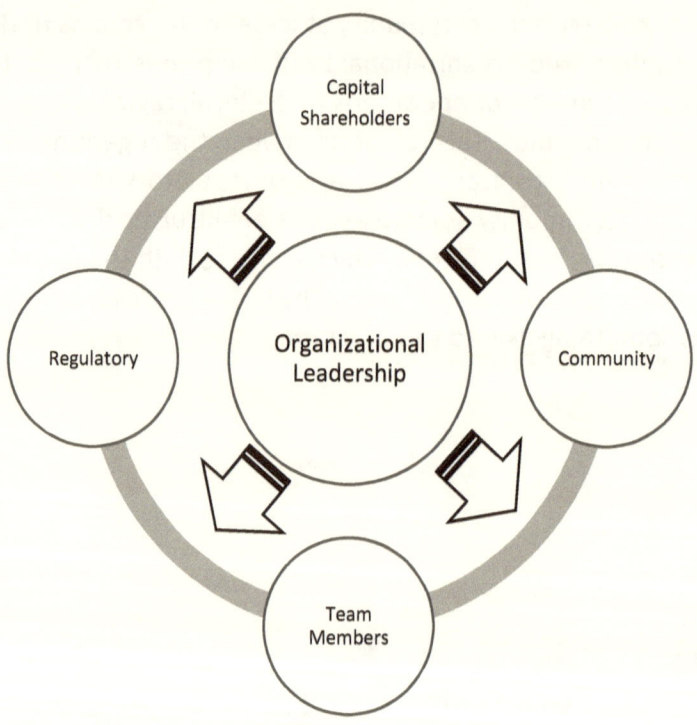

For example, if an organization needs to invest capital to assert a newly stated goal, the Organizational Leadership exchange prioritizes the relation with the shareholder's area (circle). But this priority can easily be transferred to the regulatory environment if there is a legal problem in the use or result of the use of such capital. This would mean the regulatory environment takes precedence over the shareholders.

Furthermore, the effort required to use such capital may be perceived by team members as a contrast to the reward to the team members' efforts towards the newly stated goal. This contrast must be addressed immediately, which would make the team member area (circle) the highest priority among environments.

Finally, upon noticing the new application of capital, the local community may disagree with the applicability, or social price to be paid by the capital expenditure. In this case, the organizational leaders switch primacy of priority to the community environmental issues and address the community's concern.

Therefore, all organizational leadership systems and protocols are to balance all four of these environments. Proper application of Organizational Leadership constructs assists the achievement of the stated goals. The opposite is unfortunately true. Improper design or delivery of Organizational Leadership systems will deteriorate or perhaps precipitate failure towards the stated goals.

Comparison. Synergetic Leadership is a complimentary construct of Organizational Leadership. The synergetic application towards the solution of challenges bodes well in an Organizational Leadership construct. When all participants of an organization stake claim to the delivery of the stated goals, the outcome tends to be positive. Synergy does not guarantee success but does trend extremely favorable to a better outcome than any status quo.

Contrast. There are no contrasting elements between the concept of Organizational Leadership and Synergetic Leadership. Both terms are synonymous with each other naturally. Synergetic Leadership supports Organizational Leadership. This is due to the use of cooperative efforts expected in both terms.

Conclusion. Organizational Leadership applies leader-to-team members' systems and processes to achieve the stated goals. Organizational Leadership balances four environments, which tend to interact with the Organizational Leadership as well as with each other. The four environments are the team members, the capital shareholders, the law and/or regulatory spectrum, and the social community at large. The balance between the Organizational Leadership and these four environments can dictate the likelihood or amount of success of the organization's stated goals.

19. *Paternalistic Leadership.* Dojo Sensei

Definition. Paternalistic Leadership is similar in scope and approach to Servant Leadership. (Servant Leadership will be discussed later in this chapter). The idea is the leader having a strong personal connection to the team members. A good case for Paternalistic Leadership can be made for a sensei in a dojo. Do you not speak Japanese? No problem, here is what these terms mean. A sensei is a karate master who is leading a dojo, or training center. The sensei is at a minimum a black belt, or sho-dan, which means having years of practice to attain the status of a master karate instructor. The sensei not only teaches the technical aspects of the martial arts but also leads students in the understanding of life skills which relate to the practice of karate. The relationship is similar to a father-to-child relationship in terms of the study of karate.

In Paternalistic Leadership, there is a "relationship between the leader and team members based on status orientation, involvement in issues outside the purview of work and a tendency towards directiveness" (Antonakis & Day, 2018, p. 341). The facets of Paternalistic Leadership present themselves as an inclusive way for the leader to exercise the leader-to-team member relationship.

Status orientation gives this leadership style its term. Paternal relates to the word father (Latin *paternalis*). The leader is viewed as a father figure, which consequentially makes the team member a notional offspring of the leader. Therefore, the leader interacts with the team member, or members, similar to a healthy relationship between a father and his offspring. The paternalistic leader takes the responsibility to care for the team member as a high priority. This brings us to the issue of the outside of work purview.

In a healthy father to offspring relationship, the father would be inclined to provide more than child-rearing. A father would also try to influence ancillary issues with the offspring. Issues that would normally be considered personal in nature are addressed by the paternalistic leader. Some examples may be economic distress, medical issues, or life skill deficiencies. These issues may be part of the normal leader to team member exchange. But in Paternalistic Leadership, the leader

85

may take active engagement towards the resolution of the issue.

This involvement between the paternalistic leader and the team member may become directive. In other words, the paternalistic leader may command or coerce a solution to the issue at hand autocratically. In some cases, this directiveness is regulatorily directed (company policies). But in the case of a paternalistic leader, the leader chooses the course of action unilaterally.

Before going any further, as cited earlier, do note the term Paternalistic Leadership is recognized as a leadership style derived sociologically. You can as easily substitute the term Paternalistic with Maternal, Sibling or Guardian Leadership. The term Paternalistic is used to describe the behavior and does not favor any understanding of the importance of family-related social constructs. The term Paternalistic is just the name derived by cultural paradigms, and nothing else.

Comparison. Compared with Synergetic Leadership, Paternalistic Leadership presents an opportunity for synergy between the leader and a team member. If the closeness of the relationship allows for synergetic or cooperative involvement, then Synergetic Leadership is quite compatible with Paternalistic Leadership. But this may not be the case.

Contrast. The closeness of the relationship may not allow for cooperation between parties. This may be due to the desire for directiveness by the paternalistic leader. In this case, the use of synergy is degraded to a point of losing the advantages of interpersonal cooperation. Furthermore, friction between the paternalistic leader and a team member may occur.

Conclusion. Paternalistic leadership follows a pattern derived from the general concept of a father figure. The relationship between the paternalistic leader and the team member can be conducive to bring about a positive resolution to a team member's challenge. But the directiveness tendency of this leadership style may be contraindicated. This may happen when the team member is not capable of cooperating with the paternalistic leader in a resolution of a personal challenge. The directness approach of a paternalistic leader may be an obstacle to the successful resolution of a team member's challenge.

20. *Political Leadership*. US Presidency

Definition. Political Leadership refers to leadership performed in an environment where recruitment and/or elective balloting is required for admission. A case in point would be the US presidential campaign. The mere term "political" can produce less than desirable responses to practitioners of leadership. This is because in leadership, generally speaking, a positive outcome for both the organization and the community at large is expected. In Political Leadership, there is a tendency to protect the political environments as a primacy to other priorities. Politics, as a social endeavor, has many positives and its fair share of negatives. One of the positives is political structures may be required to lead or manage organizational systems in society. The need for a section of society to manage common societal resources is required to maintain such society's viability. In this

87

context, society benefits from a political structure. These benefits bring us to the importance of Political Leadership.

Political Leadership is a trusted agent in the production of services or systems to allow the common society to prosper. When used correctly, Political Leadership becomes a catalyst for communal success. Thus, Political Leadership can be at its' core, a positive impetus of any organizational structure.

However, there are disparities in the application of Political Leadership. There can be a tendency for cronyism or nepotism. Either case attempts to solidify control at the expense of equal opportunity participation. Sometimes, Political Leadership is void of equitability due to social stigmas or social tendencies. This produces a disparity of expected priorities between the Political Leadership organization and the community it serves. An example of this phenomenon is the increase in taxes. The community may benefit from more financial resources to address the needs of such a community, but the increase in taxes affect detrimentally the community of taxpayers. This balance of needs versus cost shows one of the many challenges addressed by Political Leadership.

In Political Leadership, there is a noticeable lack of equal representation between men and women. These differentials are in part created by social norms. Some studies suggest women tend to be less attracted to political environments than men. Research suggests two causes for this phenomenon (Antonakis & Day, 2018 p. 248). Women tend to have lower self-efficacy in terms of running for political office. Secondly, men tend to be more involved in political activities as they mature from high school to college (Antonakis & Day, 2018 p. 248). The above research dates from the early decade beginning in 2000. The current political and social environments may be starting to address these anomalies.

Comparison. In the abstract, Political Leadership is highly synergetic. The understood purpose of political systems is to enhance the human experience through the application of resources to sustain and improve the way of life in societies. The effort must be synergetic. No one individual can accomplish these goals singularly. Cooperation is required to produce results in a political environment.

Contrast. There are no perfect humans. Therefore, there are no perfect leadership systems. Thus, Political Leadership has flaws. The problem with Political Leadership is disparities of representation of interests. The affinity required for the common goal of a specific Political Leadership organization tends to be at the expense of other interests. In order to combat disparities, the political environment needs to represent all team member's interests equitably for Political Leadership to perform effectively.

Conclusion. Political Leadership is the environment where the actors are either recruited or elected. These actors control the systems and resources to sustain the society the Political Leadership organization serves. Political Leadership can serve as a catalyst for the sustainment and progress of society. However, social norms and poor moral (or agreed) values deter Political Leadership to its altruistic possibilities. A good example of this disparity is the difference in participation in politics by gender. This disparity is unsustainable for future Political Leadership success.

21. *Prestige-Based Leadership.* Sport team's Captain

Definition. Prestige-based Leadership is a unique way to provide the benefits of a leader-to-team member exchange. It implies the leader provides some direction or other resources to enhance the viability of team members. In return, the team improves the status of the leader by prestige (Antonakis & Day, 2018, p. 207). As an example, in a sports team, the player who can inspire (or coerce) the team to work harder (than previously noted) may be elected, or designated, as the team Captain. This position does not come with any other monetary, or similar, compensation. For the effort provided, this player has received the prestige of being designated the team Captain. This allows the designated Captain to influence efforts both vertically upwards (toward the coaches) and vertically downwards (with fellow players). This influence is valid enough to make the moniker of Team Captain a leadership position. The entire organization (team) benefits from the effort, and the compensation for the service is the prestige of the position.

A prestige-based leader can exert authority and coerce obedience to other team members of the organization. The effectiveness of these behaviors is tenuous at best. Recall the prestige was given by demonstrated performance and should not have been earned in any other way. Thus, what was given by good performance may be lost by poor performance. The ability of the prestige-based leader to maintain the status earned is dependent upon sustained positive performance.

Comparison. Prestige-Based Leadership is highly synergetic. There is a direct connection between Synergetic Leadership and Prestige-Based Leadership. The team is motivated by the leader's input and cooperation among team members. This leader-to-team member relationship provides the prestige for the leader.

Contrast. There are issues that can derail this leader to team member exchange. The first would be a divergence of performance of the prestige-based leader. In the example before, if the team Captain underperforms as a leader, then this player loses the prestige of the position and could be substituted by another individual.

Secondly, if cronyism or nepotism occurs to receive the Prestige-Based Leadership position, then a similar situation as the aforementioned paragraph occurs. Again, the lack of expected performance leads to the removal of the prestige of the leader. Subsequently, the leader is replaced.

Conclusion. Prestige-Based Leadership is a relationship where leader actions are rewarded by leadership positions of respect or higher status, i.e. prestige. Prestige-Based leadership can be and should be, synergetic. This is because the status derived is based on the ability of the leader to coordinate a group effort towards the stated goals. There are conditions where Prestige-Based Leadership fails in its construct. Improper selection of a prestige-based leader would mean the removal and replacement of such a leader. This happens as the result of the leadership actions not meeting the desired expectations of the team.

22. *Relational Leadership.* Sports Team Manager

Definition. As the title implies, relational Leadership refers to the myriad of social interactions between the leader and a team member (or members). The success of these relationships is derived from the quality of the relationship (Antonakis & Day, 2018, p. 112). It is inferred the better the relationship between the leader and the team member(s), the better the outcome toward the stated goals. However, the quality of the relationship encompasses many elements. These elements, in the aggregate, determine the success of the leader to team member(s) relationship.

The determining factor in Relational Leadership is obviously, the quality of the relationship between the leader and the team members. It is understood leadership as a construct begins with the leader. The leader's actions are measured by the achievement of stated goals. However, leadership actions are not static. Leaders may act contextually and change leadership styles, priorities, or processes to react to changes or discrepancies of the stated goals. These leadership led changes may influence positively or negatively the quality of the leader to team members' relationship.

On the other side of the equation, even if the leader acts very consistently, the team members may react differently toward the leader by changes in perception of the relationship. For example, leaders may be having a very synergetic approach to the interaction with the team members towards the achievement of the stated goals. But processes can change, requiring new skills or information not available to the team members. When this happens, the team members may not react positively to the interaction with the leader. This is because they are not able to exchange synergetic ideas for a lack of skills or knowledge of the new paradigm.

Another limitation of the Relational Leadership environment is the constant changes in organizational goals and processes. These changes may not be favorable for the use of the current leader-to-team members' leadership processes. In such cases, the leader must adapt to a new leadership environment to accomplish the stated goals. In conjunction, the entire team must also adapt to a new approach to goal achievement. This new adaptation will involve a variation of the current Relationship Leadership style or environment.

Comparison. Seeking a cooperative environment appropriate for the successful accomplishment of the stated goals is obviously very synergetic. The concepts of Relational Leadership and Synergetic Leadership are similar. This similarity is based on the emphasis of the common constructs which involve cooperation, and mutual profitability. Relational Leadership specifically views the quality of the relationship as a catalyst for the successful accomplishment of the stated goals.

Contrast. Whereas Relational Leadership is a construct to qualify the success of the leader-to-team members' relationship, Synergetic Leadership concentrates on a different aspect. Synergetic leadership seeks cooperation among team members, specifically to address the challenges to accomplish the stated goals. Relational Leadership includes the organizational spectrum of the leader-to-team members' relationship. Synergetic Leadership does not implicitly include the organizational spectrum. Synergetic leaders concentrate on the cooperative effort of team members regardless of what organizational issues are concurrent with the synergetic effort.

Conclusion. Relational Leadership involves the methods and characteristics of the leader-to-team members'

relationship. There are three components to this relationship: ① the leader ② the team members, ③ the organizational environment. Any of these three components may change the effectiveness of the Relational Leadership climate. These changes can be positive, similar to Synergetic Leadership. Unfortunately, changes in organizational approaches can be detrimental to the relationship between the leader and the team members.

23. *Servant Leadership.* Jesus

Definition. Servant Leadership is the premier version of leadership for moral good. This title parallels the expected behavior of holy deities. It may also be referred to as Sacrificial Leadership. This sense of sacrificial effort for the good of the team members is no surprise to Christian believers. In Christianity, Servant/Sacrificial Leadership is directly attributed to Jesus. His version of servitude and sacrifice is His death on the cross for the atonement of the sins of all humans. Christians believe the acceptance of this sacrifice forgives all sins and allows salvation and participation in heaven with God.

Simply put, a servant leader always puts the interest of the organization, team members, or the stated goals ahead of the leader's personal or professional interests. Sacrificial leaders serve all three interests mentioned above ahead of themselves simultaneously. If successful, the servant leader will leave as a legacy of this leadership style. This means the servant style of leadership is at least of equal importance to the leader itself. In some cases, the Servant Leadership style is more remembered than the leader who applied its' constructs.

Comparison. Synergy can be consequential in a Servant Leadership environment. This happens when a servant leader inspires the team members to act with a servant attitude themselves. This collective and cooperative servant action then becomes synergetic. Synergy can be a desirable outcome of Servant Leadership. Servant or sacrificial efforts can be synergetic when the team members give of themselves for the common, or higher moral, good. This effort can certainly be cooperative in nature. The common thread between Servant and Synergetic leadership is the desire to accomplish a higher moral or ethical cooperative good with all team members engaged.

The common approach of moral or ethical good not transcends the accomplishment of the stated goals. Team members also benefit. Not only a stated goal is accomplished by the team, but the leader's sacrifice tends to develop a selfless desire of team members themselves.

Contrast. Servant Leadership is normally leader centric, at the peril of the leader. The ultimate servitude act is to give yourself for something other than your personal gain. In this case, a synergetic approach is not necessary for the servitude act. When Servant Leadership does not require synergy in its application, then synergy is inconsequential.

Conclusion. Servant Leadership promotes the better moral or ethical good above the needs or requirements of the leaders themselves. It requires a sacrificial effort on the part of the leader. The result of this sacrifice is a positive

95

outcome of the stated goals. The results of Servant Leadership can be synergetic if the influence of the leader inspires the team members to act with a servant attitude toward the accomplishment of the stated goals.

24. *Shared Leadership*. Law Firm Partnership

Definition. Shared leadership is a process where the leadership role is transferred between members of a group intentionally (Antonakis & Day, 2018, p. 169). This transferal, or shift, occurs with purpose. The purpose of this shift is needed due to the changing environment in which the group is operating, or a change in circumstances to achieve the stated goals. A hybrid of the two conditions may also occur.

Think of Shared Leadership in an Attorney Law Firm. Within the firm, some attorneys specialize in different aspects of the practice of law. In one case, a client seeks legal help in a wrongful death case, then attorneys who specialize in these types of cases take the leadership responsibilities for the case. Another client may have a contract dispute, which will be handled by other attorneys of the firm who deal with contractual issues. The legal need of the clients determines who leads the client's case. Leadership is shared between attorneys by the legal need of the clients.

This type of leadership is counterintuitive to the norm of hierarchy in leadership roles. Normally, the leaderships constructs begin or are centered in an individual who exercises the leadership, or leadership related actions. The leader may address environmental or circumstantial issues by delegating the responsibility of resolution to a team member. However, the leader retains the authority and accountability for the achievement of the stated goals.

In a Shared Leadership environment, actors may bring different sets of knowledge and skills unique to them. This unique input is required for the overall achievement of the stated goals. So, when a specific skill set is required in a specific process to accomplish the specific stated organizational goals, the individual with a specific set of skills assumes the leadership role. When a new environmental or process challenge emerges, the individual best suited for the leadership of this specific area replaces the former leader. This protocol continues until the stated goals are achieved.

It should be of no surprise the use of Shared Leadership improves self-efficacy and skill development of group members in the leadership environment (Antonakis & Day, 2018 p. 177). When responsibility and accountability are directed to an individual, there is normally a positive response towards the challenge. Furthermore, Shared Leadership models become a better predictor of variance outcomes than hierarchical leadership models (Antonakis & Day, 2018, p. 177). This means that when you use Shared Leadership models, it is easier to account for variances in the expected result than in hierarchical leadership styles.

Comparison. Clearly, Shared Leadership is highly synergetic. The cooperation is related to the individual specific skills, and the willingness to share the status of leader in the pursuit of the stated goals. To make Shared Leadership work, synergy must be a component, since a lack of lateral cooperation between actors would not, by definition, be synergetic.

Contrast. Simply said, Shared Leadership requires a different view of leadership roles when compared to other hierarchical leadership models. The application of the concept of Shared Leadership requires a special set of requirements. These requirements may not be readily deliverable due to the culture, structure, or human resource systems of the organization. The idiomatic "think outside the box" paradigm shift is required. However, if the organization can shift the culture and processes to a Shared Leadership centric environment, then the organization will benefit from the advantages derived from this leadership model.

Conclusion. Shared Leadership is a goal achievement process model where leaders shift hierarchical control intentionally. The environment or circumstances act as a catalyst for change for the recognized leader. This change is formal. There are distinct advantages to operate in a Shared Leadership model. There is better self-efficacy of actors and better performance from shared leaders. However, the implementation of the Shared Leadership model requires a shift from a hierarchical leadership model. Shared leadership by nature is very synergetic and complements the Synergetic Leadership model.

25. *Situational Leadership.* School Teacher

Definition. In Situational Leadership, the actual operational environment dictates the leader's behavior and the stated goal outcome (Antonakis & Day, 2018, p. 146). It is sort of "going with the flow leadership." The leader adjusts the leadership style used in the context of the environment. The outcome becomes a variable that is modified by the leader. This modification is based on the circumstances.

Successful teachers practice Situational Leadership. The concept of learning is not static. There is no "one way" to teach. Teachers may have to adapt to the learning skills of each individual student. Simple concepts for a group of students may require a different approach with another set of students. The measure of teaching is not what is presented by the teacher, but what is learned by the student. Therefore, the teacher may have to adapt to the student's cognitive abilities in order to teach a subject matter.

It is natural to expect the leader to modify the approaches used based on the current situation. Idiomatically speaking, "you've got to scour (plow) with the hoe given" (unknown authored idiom). The leader must adapt resources and processes unique to the situation at hand. This environment bodes well for adaptable and process malleable leaders. This environment is detrimental to individuals who are incapable of flexible adaptation.

Like any other leadership style, Situational Leadership is simply trying to achieve the organizational stated goals. The contextual issue is the constant variation of the environment. Situational leaders modify the leadership constructs to achieve success in this environment.

Comparison. Situational Leadership is compatible and symbiotic to Synergetic Leadership. A situational leader seeks whatever resource needed to assert a resolution towards the situation at hand. This desire to solve issues with other trends toward synergetic behaviors. In Synergetic Leadership, cooperation is presumed. In Situational Leadership, cooperation is one of many components in the strategy to deal with the changing issues.

Contrast. Situational Leadership does not require synergy if the competence of the leader is very high. If such is the case, theoretically, the leader simply makes changes to the approach to the situation unilaterally. However, it is doubtful a leader will be able to cope with constant changes without the cooperation of the team itself. Furthermore, challenges and changes do affect the team also. It would be beneficial for the leader to seek cooperation for a situational solution. But again, synergy may not be necessary or available due to the situation at hand.

Conclusion. Situational Leadership is applied in an environment where a leader must understand the parameters and outcomes of continually occurring changes. The leader adapts the leadership styles and modes to accomplish the stated goals of the enterprise. The fact Situational Leadership involves cooperation between many organizational processes that make this style synergistically compatible. However, it is necessary for the situational leader to adapt to changes in conditions for the accomplishment of the stated goals.

26. *Strategic Leadership.* Company Board of Directors

Definition. Simply said, Strategic Leadership involves the greater scope of influences in and out of the organization. It is similar in scope to Organizational Leadership. It is functional, in that it coordinates functions to align with external environments (Antonakis & Day, 2108, p. 7).

Who practices these types of Leadership? Think of individuals who look at the proverbial "big picture". A good example is the Company Board of Directors. These individuals are responsible for the short-term and long-term goals of the company. These individuals discuss and plan the actions required by the company to expand, succeed and profit from the current and future business environments. The Bottom line is Strategic Leaders look at the "big picture" of "how we got here" and "what are we going to do next".

In Strategic Leadership, the leaders formulate the processes and protocols to deal with the expectations of external environments. Recall this chart from Organizational Leadership.

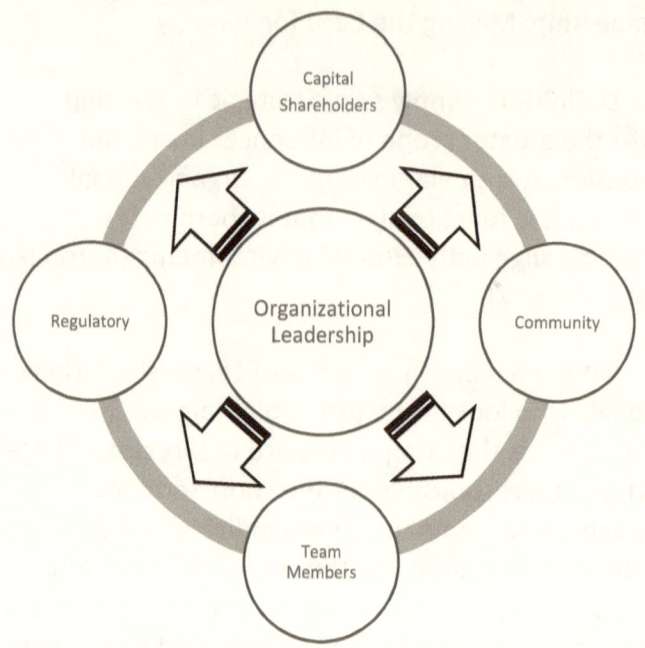

In Strategic Leadership, the organization is interacting laterally with regulations (government-centric) and the community at large (clients, users, non-governmental organizations, media and its' derivatives, etc.). Strategic leaders foment strategies to deal laterally and simultaneously with the plethora of external forces. These external forces do exert pressure on the organization by creating an expectation of results complementary to the political and social environments. In addition, and again simultaneously, the strategic leaders must comply with the expectation of the shareholders, since they provide the capital for the organization to exist in the first place. Furthermore, strategic leaders deal with future challenges for team members to solve.

All these practices and processes must be developed, coordinated, and implemented with cohesiveness across the organization. There cannot be any acceptable failure by part of the consortium of strategic programs. Is so, the organizational goal can be affected detrimentally.

Comparison. Strategic and Synergetic Leadership go hand in hand. By the nature of complex, and perhaps a large amount of data, systems, and individuals affected, the need for intra and outer cooperation is understood. A strategic leader needs a synergetic relationship among members of the organization. These organizational members provide the impetus of achievement for the intra-organizational goals. Strategic leaders also need to engage synergistically with external actors to comply with external organizational expectations and achieve the stated goals of the organization.

Contrast. There is no notable contrast observed between the Strategic Leadership environment and the Synergetic Leadership environment. Synergetic Leadership can be applied in both the inter-organizational spectrum, as well as outside of the organization. The main difference is which actors are being engaged in synergetic activities.

Conclusion. Strategic Leadership deals with the complex and sometimes large set of programs to achieve the stated goals of an organization. These strategic programs can be internal or external to the organization. The cooperation among a large set of actors makes Strategic Leadership very synergetic. Synergy is required among all strategic leaders to achieve the organizational stated goals.

27. *Transactional Leadership*. Sales Associate

103

Definition. Basically, Transactional Leadership follows the profile of economic exchange (Antonakis & Day, 2018, p. 62). This economic exchange follows the "quid pro quo" scenario. In theory, it is good faith depended. This is to say, if the transactional leader provides a good to the team or team member, then the latter reciprocates to the leader with the desired result (stated goals). The reverse could also be true. A leader valued transaction initiated by a team member (or the team itself), would be in turn rewarded by positive actions from the transactional leaders.

The classical example of this is a commission sales associate. The more this individual sells, the more compensation is received. The leader then may provide extra incentives for specific sales achievements, which incentivize the sales associate to work even harder.

In Transactional Leadership, good faith in the relationship is required. This is the difference between good and bad transactions. Think of the often-maligned car dealership salesmen. The salesman is providing a vehicle (new or used), and the client expects the exchange to be fair and in good faith for the price paid. This would be a positive exchange of resources, money for the car.

However, either party can negatively affect the transaction. The dealer may fail to inform the client of known anomalies in the car's performance. The client can fail to make the payments for the automobile. In either of these two cases, the transaction is negative.

In hierarchical leadership models, the leader initiates actions with the team. Therefore, it is expected for the leader to have good faith and a high level of ethical standards when performing Transactional Leadership. The exchange is contingent upon the behavior of the leader.

Comparison. Synergetic Leadership is a neutral attribute of the basic definition of Transactional Leadership. The cooperation between team members and leaders is contractual. There may be synergy among team members to ensure the accomplishment of the stated goals, but synergy is not considered by a transactional leader per se. There is no opposition in using the synergy between a leader and their team, but it is the quality of the exchange that is pursued first.

Contrast. As mentioned above, although Synergetic Leadership can easily run parallel to the use of Transactional Leadership, the latter is not a construct where synergy is sought or expected. This does not mean synergetic exchanges do not occur in the implementation of Transactional Leadership. It does mean that synergetic exchanges occur as a corollary event in Transactional Leadership.

Conclusion. Transactional Leadership follows a similar pattern to an economic exchange. The parties (leaders and team members) are poised to receive a benefit from the exchange initiated by the leader. Transactional Leadership is leader centric. The exchanges can be positive or negative, depending on the result of the exchange.

28. *Transformational Leadership*. Jeff Bezos

Definition. A concise definition of Transformational Leadership for practical use is almost impossible to contrive. It is a style of leadership that changes the leader to team member relations from simply stated goal centric to end value-centric. Quoting from previous work, Antokanis & Day state this leadership as "inducing followers to act for certain goals that represent the values and motivation, the wants and needs, the aspiration and expectations, of both leaders and followers" (Antonakis & Day, 2018, p. 65). Furthermore, the main concern of transformational leadership is the end values. (Antonakis & Day, 2018, p. 66).

The creation and development of Amazon reflect Transformational Leadership well. Mr. Jeff Bezos has created not only a profitable company but a new dynamic in the procurement of all types of commodities via internet sales. His vision has made consumer acquisition of goods a simple and convenient process. In only requires a mobile device and you can order just about anything and have it delivered where you are. Mr. Bezos has transformed how we buy goods. The value of simplicity and convenience permeates how the team members deliver customer satisfaction.

As Amazon has shown, in practice, Transformational Leadership is not only concerned with the stated goals of the organization. This leadership style incorporates an altruistic value to what is intended to be the stated goal. For example, a manufacturing leader is obviously concerned with the production of a certain type of "gizmo." If the manufacturing leader is practicing Transformational Leadership, then, not only must the "gizmo" be produced efficiently, but the production of the "gizmo" must have the expected value to leadership and equal value to the team members.

The team members are motivated to perform well by several factors. These include identifying and articulating a vision, providing an appropriate model, fostering the acceptance of group goals, communicating high-performance expectations, providing individualized support and being intellectually stimulating (Antonakis & Day, 2018, p. 67).

The key component is the desire for Transformational Leadership to be a construct to produce a better "good." It is sort of an altruistic enhancement of the stated goals. The goodness of the leader is reciprocated with the goodness of team members. This, in turn, produces a stated goal that is organically good.

Comparison. As expected, the components in the definition of Synergetic Leadership buttress nicely with Transformational Leadership. Recall, this book makes the case for leadership to be Human Applied Synergy. The word "human" is used to describe the positive effect of the result of a leadership construct. Applied synergy, or the application of synergy, is to be understood as a cooperative effort to solve a challenge. Therefore, the Synergetic Leadership process attempts to improve a human condition with a cooperative effort. Transformational Leadership makes a similar attempt, but the methodology is related to the good faith intentions of the leader toward a general betterment of the stated goals.

Contrast. The differences between Transformational Leadership and Synergetic Leadership are related mostly to methodology. The desire for an outcome beneficial to the leadership and team member exchange is expected in both leadership styles. Transformational Leadership centers on expecting a higher value for both the leader and team members. Synergetic Leadership is mostly centered on the process of cooperation as the impetus for success.

Conclusion. Transformational Leadership sets the value for both leader and team members as a centric goal. It is assumed this value is good or altruistic. This value is obtained by the inspirational emphasis of the leader. The Transformational Leader is assumed to be "good" and leads with this altruistic mindset. Transformational Leadership coincides with Synergetic Leadership as both seek positive outcomes toward the stated goals by cooperative effort. The difference is in the impetus. In Transformational Leadership, the impetus is the goodness of the leader and the leadership goals. In Synergetic Leadership, the positive outcome is derived from cooperative effort.

29. *Transformational-Transactional Leadership.* Robert E. Lee

Definition. The term Transformational-Transactional Leadership is, as the name implies, a hybrid of both previously described leadership styles. This hybrid includes some elements of the two leadership styles. Borrowing from the Transactional Leadership model, roles and task requirements behaviors are included in this hybrid model. From a more contemporary school of leadership, such as Transformational Leadership, elements like vision are included (Antonakis & Day, 2018, p. 66). What is attempted to be described is a leadership style that encompasses an entire spectrum of behaviors and processes to create a workable leadership style.

Robert E. Lee is an example of the attributes of a Transformational-Transactional Leader. The highest commanding officer of the Confederate Army during the US Civil War demonstrated both leadership styles. From the Transactional Leadership standpoint, General Lee exchanged the need for adherence to his directed military strategy and tactics for the army to receive success on the battlefield. As a Transformational Leader, General Lee centered the army's vision on the idea of defending the homeland and loving the South's traditional way of life.

It is assumable the combination of "the best of both worlds" bodes well as a practical implementation of a leadership style. The problem of making such an assertion is measurable analytics. The measurement of analytics on a hybrid system does not equate to a better understanding of the attempted leadership style. In other words, the hybrid style can lead the research away from the known favorable factors asserted and imbedded in each original leadership style.

This leads academia with the distinct duty to further research the attributes of the hybrid (Transformational-Transactional) model style. From research, three possibilities may arise. First, research may conclude that indeed the hybrid system provides a better construct to either singular system. Or, research may chide the notion of the hybrid system as a better leadership construct. In addition, research may find the hybrid system may trend towards a different

109

path for the accomplishment of stated goals. Only time and research will tell.

Comparison. The Transformational-Transactional Leadership style has synergetic aspects. By the inclusion of Transactional Leadership style, synergy can be available as a means to the end of the stated goals' accomplishment. Furthermore, the inclusion of the Transformational Leadership style, where cooperative vision is lauded, synergy is also exercised to accomplish the stated goals. Therefore, synergy is normally a part of this hybrid leadership style.

Contrast. The contrast between Transformational-Transactional Leadership styles and Synergetic leadership is mostly about processes, and not philosophical. Both the hybrid model and synergetic styles are dependent upon the willful cooperation of the team in general. Synergetic Leadership makes this cooperation the core value of the premise. The Transformational-Transactional model includes synergetic elements for the successful accomplishment of the stated goals, but synergy is not the core element. In the hybrid model, synergy is consequential to the input of the leader.

Conclusion. Transformational-Transactional leadership style is a hybrid of two styles. One (Transactional) is "old school," relating to the relationship of roles and tasks between the leader and team members. The other style (Transformational) is a contemporary style where attributes such as vision and inspiration center the team effort. This hybrid attempts to describe and employ the best leadership elements of the two individual styles. These elements do coincide with the concept of Synergetic Leadership. Although the hybrid nature of this style shows great potential, to provide full acceptance of the term, more research is required.

30. *Vertical Leadership.* Totem Poles

Definition. Vertical Leadership is easy to understand. It follows the Northwest American indigenous tribe hierarchy. This hierarchy is displayed on Totem Poles, where faces of individuals are carved, one on top of the other. The higher the face portrayal on the pole, the higher the honor status.

Similarly, Vertical Leadership is sort like a Totem Pole. The leaders are of the top, and the rest of the team is underneath of the leader in order of status. In this construct, it would be easy to conclude the lowest individual on the pole does not enjoy the benefits of the leadership structure. Surprisingly, this is not the case.

Research of Vertical Leadership has concluded this leadership style both "serves as a facilitating force for smooth social interactions" and "directly affects the group's ability to *share* (author emphasis added) leadership effectively" (Antokanis & Day, 2018, p. 174).

The key element required in Vertical Leadership is trust. A good (read trustworthy) vertical leader will facilitate shared leadership modalities and activities among team members. This foments the cooperative effort to accomplish

111

the stated goals. When the relationship between Vertical Leadership and Shared Leadership is analyzed based on research, the conclusion is synergistically positive. Research has "identified the important role that vertical leadership has in the display and development of shared leadership" (Antonakis & Day, 2018, p. 175).

Comparison. The connection between the "Totem Pole" Vertical Leadership and Shared Leadership model is very synergetic. When the vertical leader uses this style correctly, the team members do perform in a very cooperative approach to the accomplishment of the stated goals. Shared leadership presumes a synergetic effort between elements providing input toward stated goals' success.

Contrast. Vertical Leadership performed by a trustworthy leader may, as stated earlier, lead to a cooperative effort. However, because Vertical Leadership only describes the direction of the impetus from top to bottom, it is easy to see how the misuse of the direction of impetus could lead to despotic behavior. This behavior would not be synergetic. Therefore, Synergetic Leadership is a process dependent and presumed altruistically. Vertical leadership can be synergetic, but can also not be so. This is because synergy is not the primary consideration of a vertical leader. The vertical leader is a facilitator and not a synergistic motivator per se.

Conclusion. Vertical leadership is by design the relationship top to bottom between the leader and the team members. Trustworthy vertical leaders may subsequently tend to a Shared Leadership model. The vertical leader's trust of the team members is a key element. When the vertical leader trusts the team, shared models of leadership can be developed. Shared Leadership is by definition synergetic because the shared modality assumes cooperation between actors. However, this synergy is only available when the vertical leader does foment trust among the organization led.

Overall Summary.

The 30 leadership terms shown in this chapter are not an all-inclusive list of leadership related concepts. But recall the contextual reason for this book. It is a practical guide for the successful utilization of leadership concepts. These concepts are centered around the case being made that synergy is the central theme, and outcome, of a leadership endeavor. Therefore, all 30 leadership terms were compared with the concept of cooperative success understood as synergy.

What follows in the next 7 chapters are practical applications to the concept of Synergetic Leadership. These practical lessons and guides will assist the practitioner of Synergetic Leadership to effectively achieve the stated goals of their respective organization.

Chapter 3
Synergetic Leadership vs. Management

"Who's on first?" (Abbott and Costello comedy routine)

It is common to hear individuals of all walks of life discuss management and leadership, sometimes at the same time. This creates a confusing exchange. There is a conundrum between leadership and its relativity to the concept of management or vice versa. This conundrum takes many forms, but it generally comes down to delineating the primacy or hierarchy between the two disciplines. Hence the Abbott and Costello reference: "Who's on first (base)?" or in the case of leadership vs. management, which is the centerpiece concept between the two?

Business school candidates seem to favor the position leadership is an attribute of a model manager. The latter uses leadership to enhance managerial expectations. Naturally, this model flows over to the practitioners of management. If such an individual earns an academic degree in management, it is easy to understand the natural tendency to view leadership as a subset, or attribute of an ideal manager or management practices. But of course, there is a dissenting view brought up by other leadership practitioners such as military officers and high rankings noncommission officers (sergeants).

Leadership students and practitioners normally advocate and practice the reverse notion of the management

114

centric primacy. To a leadership practitioner, (i.e. and individual who practices leadership as the main part of their job) management skills are an attribute to be used to achieve the team's stated goals. This is very true in the military. In the military construct, leadership is more valued than management as it pertains to achieving the stated goals. Military minded individuals do value immensely the idea of managing resources. However, military leaders mostly believe good management practices are an attribute of a competent leader.

Further confusing the debate, managers and leadership practitioners sometimes use the terms management and leadership as synonyms, or interchangeably. This is especially true when discussing teams, or team leaders and team members. For example, the head authority in the field of play in a baseball team is called a manager. Sometimes players for this manager are referred to as great leaders among the team. In this role, a player exercises excellent motivational skills to improve the outcome of games. If true, this notion presents an interesting question. Why didn't the manager conduct such motivation? Is it not the purview of the manager to lead the team? The answer is that in this case motivation, leadership and management are being used interchangeably to denote a successful approach to winning.

There are similarities in both concepts of management and leadership. The best one-phrase description of similarities is this: Both management and leadership *"Make things happen."* The major dissimilarity is the emphasis on what is the centerpiece of each discipline. In management, resource utilization is the centerpiece of success. This emphasis does include the personnel assigned. Generally speaking, in leadership, human performance is the emphasis of effort. Yet, resource allocation (other than personnel) does play a part in the success measured in a leadership construct.

Thus, the specific task to explain and advocate for an answer to the "management vs. leadership" primacy enigma is left to be solved. In order to do so, some segmentation of the terms is required. The concept of management will be discussed first.

Management

Setting aside the technical or academic definitions of management, we begin the management versus leadership discussion of what is to be accomplished by management. For the purposes of this book, management is defined as the efficient allocation and operation of resources. These resources are materials, non-living systems and lifeforms (flora, fauna, and humans). Materials or real assets are those things that are accountable. These could include raw materials, such as water, wood, minerals, houses, cars, and money. The interaction is one-way, the raw materials do not care and are unaware of the disposition of themselves. These items are handled unilaterally by the manager, with the only restrictions of such management is the result expected, or the artificial regulatory limitations on the managerial extent of control. The subordinates of the manager are affected directly or indirectly by the control of the materials, but this follows the last managed segment which will be explained later.

Systems are also managed. These can be engineering systems, artificially intelligent systems, or peripheral systems operating cooperatively. The manager controls these systems to provide the products or services the systems were designed to create. As it was with materials (or assets) management, there is no managerial human consequence to the use of these systems (other than what the systems are programmed to accomplish). Again, there are reactions between managers and

116

subordinates (team members) operating the systems, but not with the systems per se. Lifeforms are the next category of management resources.

Lifeforms are also managed. In the non-human spectrum of management, flora and fauna are managed by humans. In the flora department, whole plant ecosystems are managed to provide the best use of this resource, for sustainability and profit. Flora reacts to management by producing the desired result. Good flora management results in good plant product yields.

Fauna is also managed to produce some type of yield. Zookeepers manage their animals to ensure a healthy population for the discovery, education, and enjoyment of the zoo visitors. Cattle, pig and chicken farmers manage their stocks to yield protein (and other products) for human consumption. Wildlife managers manage the environment to ensure the sustainability of wildlife in the area of the manager's responsibility. It is well understood that animals feel and can be emotionally affected by human interaction. This part of fauna managing does have a leadership inclination. The manager which directly or indirectly controls a fauna group can manage the respective group for better use of this resource. But under the synergetic definition of leadership, fauna is not led per se because the first condition in the definition of synergetic leadership is human interaction.

The last category of lifeforms is humans. Managers do interact with humans. Managers interact with subordinates, co-manager, supervisors and peripheral team members. The efficient allocation or operation of resources is the goal of management. However, the manner of the utilization of human resources takes secondary importance to productivity achieved. In other words, productivity achieved is more

117

important than the way the team members achieved the result. In the management construct, leadership is a way for humans to be managed. This is to say leadership is embedded in the operational aspects of management. Leadership, and Synergetic Leadership, in particular attempts to extract the best possible results of the stated goals by energizing the team efforts towards the goals. Leadership puts a premium on how to achieve success with the human component. This is where the definitions and importance of management and leadership diverge. With this divergence in mind, we now explore the contrast between management and leadership.

Leadership

As stated in the preface chapter, the goal of this book is to define, in a practical way, what leadership is based on the concept of synergy. It is assumed the interactions of leadership are human-centric. Thus, for the purpose of this book leadership is defined as *Human Applied Synergy*. There are interactions in other life forms where cooperation does enhance the survival and other beneficial aspects of the group. However, a leader of an animal pack is not necessarily applying leadership concepts. A leader of the pack asserts instinct.

Materials do not interact with each other unless forced by organically natural actions or human intervention. Materials are not led. Thus, there is no leadership involved with materials. This is because the objects do not respond with human qualities as to the actions exerted on them. Whether a rock moves or does not, is irrelevant to the rock. To a miner, it is quite different. The ore miner wishes and expects the rock to move. But not the rock; it is lifeless.

Systems are not led either. Even the most complex artificial intelligence systems are only as sophisticated as the programmer allows it to be. Artificial intelligence does apply synergy to collect and analyze the ever-increasing amount of

118

data available. But this synergy is artificial, again, the result of a specific programming code provided by the system programmer, (perhaps a manager). The same can be said about engineering systems. These are controlled by engineering processes installed and monitored by engineering-centric personnel. The systems may interact with other engineering or artificial intelligence systems but do so at the specific programming of the developer.

Recall in the management resource section, the next tier of management is flora, fauna, and humans. Flora and fauna follow synergetic actions based on protocols or instincts for survival. Sequoia trees interlock their roots to provide mutual structural support to the affected trees. Wolves and lions (among others) hunt in packs to increase the possibility of a meal to be trapped and consumed. This is an instinct that evolved in countless generations. Yet the motivation is related to survival, a basic life requirement. This is not a human-directed leadership input per se. This leaves us with the human factor.

Humans are led. The discourse of this book tries to assert that when two individuals are together attempting to complete a stated goal, one of them is led. This is true regardless of the size of the group. The leadership action is applied by using synergy, or a form of synergy thereof. Leadership is a human phenomenon because it is not applied just for the mere survival of a human group. Leadership is used for all kinds of endeavors to improve the status quo or the stated goal. Leadership is a higher need than just survival. Leadership is expected to improve the human experience itself.

So back to the original question: Who's on first?

The primacy between management or leadership, as it pertains to the accomplishment of the stated goals, depends on what assets are being considered. Management takes primacy when the items managed are either material, systems, or non-human living things. These items are managed to extract or produce the required resources for use or consumption by humans. Materials, systems and non-human living things are not led because the interaction and the leadership construct either do not apply to the item or are/is inconsequential to the items. To quote an idiom, "If you try to teach a pig to fly, you are wasting your time and annoying the pig!". You can easily substitute the word "teach" with "lead", and the axiom would still read true.

To address the primacy between either concept, the next issue is which of the two (leadership vs. management) is more complex. This statement is riddled with interpretation dissonance. Managers could argue that the volume and differential modalities of managed items are more complex than leadership acting on humans, and only humans. This is to say managers interact with more things than leaders, who interact only with humans. Managers do exercise control over human resources in addition to managing non-human resources. Advantage managers.

Leaders can take this same argument backward, sort of a retort by reverse engineering. Leaders do concentrate their efforts in the application of maximum synergetic output from the individuals led. However, leaders do engage in managerial actions, similar to managers stated above. The difference then becomes what is the focus between leaders and managers. Leaders must focus on people; managers may focus on people. When managing or leading is viewed by the prism of the human experience, leadership may take a slight edge in this category. Advantage leaders.

120

This brings us to the discussion of which discipline requires more effort or is more difficult to exercise. This is an impossible argument to settle because it would be necessary to agree upon what "more difficult" means, and what standard of effort is being compared. In this issue, there can be no clear primacy selection.

There is only one aspect where a clear distinction between management and leadership can be derived. The distinction between management and leadership may come down to human life. If the consequence for failure is, or could be, loss of life, then whatever function is being measured takes primacy over all other functions. In military combat operations, loss of life is directly interrelated with leadership. However, not all military leaders are combat leaders exercising leadership.

Managers may make decisions where improperly managed resources create havoc to include loss of life. Think of improperly managed pharmaceutical controls in a hospital or pharmacy. Such incompetence could result in loss of life, and no leadership construct was being directly used.

The debate between the primacy of leadership and management boils down to the human component. Suppose a manager is managing asset systems with direct consequences to humans. If a managerial failure would likely mean loss of life, then management takes a primacy role. In this case, leadership becomes an operational attribute of the management construct.

On the reverse side, if the execution of a stated goal is such that inappropriate leadership applied could result in loss of life, then leadership is the primary component to success. In this case, management becomes an attribute under the leadership umbrella. As an example, think of a lead fire chief in a fire event involving a large structure with victims inside. This leader must be able to lead multiple teams of firefighters to rescue affected personnel and avoid the proliferation of the fire. Failure could result in loss of life (victims or firefighters) in addition to further destruction of structures.

Finally, perhaps it is irrelevant which concept takes on primacy over the other. There are so many complex constructs where both concepts are used, that determining the primacy of either concept becomes useless. Managers may lead and leaders need to be good managers.

A fast-food restaurant manager oversees the use of products (food) as well as personnel (employees). Yet failure in managing the employees can result in human failure (food poisoning). This manager acts as a leader to ensure the proper use and processes for food preparation are achieved by all employees involved. The manager is also leading.

Military leaders and First Responder leaders are both directly responsible for the actions of subordinates in the achievement of their respective stated goals, normally involving human life. These leaders also have to care for the administration of human resource issues, a typical managerial function. These leaders are also providing managerial actions.

Thus, the manager may lead, leaders may manage. The only derivative of the management versus leadership primacy is the importance of the human element. Whether humans in an organization are being managed or lead, the important factor is to assert the correct discipline for the benefit of the human component of the organization. This is, of course, accomplished at par with the stated group goals.

Chapter 4

Synergetic Leadership Attributes

"Pretty is as pretty does" Common English idiom

As stated in the preface, this book is intended for practical applications. In this chapter, the most critical attributes necessary for excellent Synergetic Leadership dynamics will be presented. These attributes are the cornerstone of the practice of Synergetic Leadership. The list is intentionally short. Using an entire catalog of leadership centric attributes would make this book very long. This is to say the attributes presented in this chapter are not an all-inclusive list to the Synergetic Leadership model. In addition, the attributes presented are also common to other leadership styles and are also common to management desired skills. Yet, these attributes were chosen as the keystones to develop or enhance a Synergetic Leadership model.

Therefore, a practitioner of leadership, and specifically a synergetic leader, will benefit from a shortlist of attributes to utilize. It makes the addressing of required attributes manageable. If you are a leader already having and using any of the attributes presented, then little change is required in the way Synergetic Leadership is to be applied. However, if any of the attributes are deficient or missing, the leadership practitioner will benefit in understanding what attributes are

123

required for success in Synergetic Leadership. Presented below are seven of the keystone attributes for a synergetic leader. Incidentally, some of these attributes will also be discussed in greater detail in chapter 5.

Trust (Trusted Agent) & Loyalty. Trust is crucial to the practitioner of leadership, and especially Synergetic Leadership. This is because being a trusted agent is the "glue" that keeps the interactions between leadership and team members active. Trust can generally be defined as the confidence of integrity between two (or more) parties. One member of the group can count on the other member to act in a principled way, devoid of actions contrary to the benefit of the relationship.

In Synergetic Leadership, the main focus is the cooperation of members of the group to bring the best solutions towards the stated goals. Trust, and its applicable human model, trusted agent, ensures the participants working towards the stated goals are the center of the synergetic exercise, and nothing else. A trusted agent, especially as a leader, must be able to ensure the valued interests of the team are protected individually, and as a whole.

The criticality of the trusted agent's behavior comes to bear when things do not go as planned. Members of the team must have confidence in the leader to protect the interest of team members regardless of the achievement of stated goals. If the stated goals are not achieved or are partially achieved, the leaders will address the issue with no detriment to the individual morale of team members, or the team as a whole. Behaviors and deficiencies would be addressed to ensure the achievement of future stated goals, but the relationship between team members and their leader remains intact. This is not to say there may be negative consequences to errors or non-compliance towards the stated goals. But the trusted agent will react to the discrepancy, and not on the team member's persona.

This brings us to the subject of loyalty. Loyalty is referred to as affection or attachment. The team member(s) may feel loyalty towards the leader. Sometimes loyalty is confused with the concept of trust. This confusion usually arises when the team member confuses professional loyalty with personal loyalty. Using the idea of loyalty as a feeling of attachment, professional loyalty is expected and required by both parties (leader and member) mutually. It is part of the leader-to-team member exchange. This attachment is regardless of the personal feelings of either party. The team member may not like the leader, or vice-versa. However, the stated goals of the organization require both entities to work together for the benefit of the team, and the overall organization. The leader does not earn or need to earn, the team member's professional loyalty. Professional loyalty is required for participation and rewards of the team's stated goals. Therefore, a trusted agent is professionally loyal to the individuals affected by the relationship, regardless of any personal feelings. The trusted agent provides the confidence of acting in the best interest of the individual team member and the stated goals. Professional loyalty is required for success and takes primacy to personal loyalty.

Personal loyalty can be a force multiplier. Personal loyalty is a sense of attachment in a positive relationship. This loyalty is earned by both the leader and the team members. The leader may enjoy personal loyalty with a team member, or members, by exercising a positive mental attitude and a team member-centric focus. Team members can enjoy personal loyalty by approaching the leader as a positive influence on the stated goals. In either case, personal loyalty is earned.

Therefore, professional loyalty is given by the leadership construct, personal loyalty is earned by the trust. Thus, as it pertains to Synergetic Leadership, a synergetic leader/trusted agent is required to have professional loyalty to the team. This is a requirement for success toward the stated goals and is generally non-negotiable.

The synergetic leader/trusted agent can enhance the synergy of the team by earning the teams' personal loyalty. Although not a requirement of success, having the teams' personal loyalty enhances the team's cohesiveness and participation toward the stated goals. This is because there is a removal of the barrier created by interpersonal friction. The latter produces some restrictions to open communications. A synergetic leader who has garnered personal loyalty may receive inputs that otherwise would be held but for the lack of trust by the team member. It's like a daughter telling a dad his tie clashes with the rest of an assemble. The daughter trusts dad will take the critique as a positive outcome (better dressed).

Either by personal or professional loyalty (or preferably both), a trust allows for open communication between the leader and team members without fear of retribution. This does not mean the leader is sided with any team members. What this does mean is the leader will do what is right and in the best interest of the team, even when no one is watching. This brings the discussion to the next attribute, integrity. Being a trusted agent and having integrity does go "hand in hand" with a synergetic leader.

Integrity. Perhaps the best description of integrity is "doing what's right when no one is looking". The need for a synergetic leader to behave with utmost integrity is acutely important since integrity is the measurement of being a trusted agent. The two terms (trusted agent and integrity) are analogous to always doing the right thing. When the team

126

understands and operates under the leader's trust and integrity, there is an improvement in the effort. This is due to the team not needing to analyze the "why" of the leader's actions.

It is necessary to point out that integrity is reciprocal, the colloquial "two-way" street. The team members are required to adhere to the same standard of trust and integrity of the leaders. One-way employment or practice of either term will not work. If the leader has little integrity, then the team will not perceive the gain or need to act with little or any integrity. This environment leads to actions that undermine the focus of team goals. Cheating with data or solutions may disrupt the synergy of the group. The leader then loses the confidence (trust) in the group, which in turn may erode the team's ability to think and operate synergistically.

The team's lack of integrity may mean the leader may not receive the benefits of synergy among team members. The corrective action of this environment is the leader's responsibility. The leader must identify the actions taken which breached the concept of the individual or team integrity. The undesirable actions need to be corrected and the team (or team member) must accept a change in behavior.

The good news is leaders who operate with the utmost integrity and behave consistently as a trusted agent seem to fare better than otherwise possible. Both being a trusted agent and behaving with utmost integrity have an emulating effect on team members. In simple terms, from the team members' perspective is this idiom: "Boss got our back and we got her/his." This relationship tends to humble the leader, which brings up the next attribute, humility.

Humility. In chapter 8, Zinger #10 the relationship between humility and Strategic Leadership is explained. (What's a Zinger? …, wait until Chapter 8). There is no need to expound much on the desirability of a synergetic leader to be a humble individual. At issue is where the leader's impetus is centered. Is the leader emphasizing leadership and its positive result? Or is the leader looking for self-serving glory and recognition?

A true synergetic leader or any excellent leader per se, rallies and rejoices around the team's achievement. The Stanley Cup (US National Hockey team overall winner) is hoisted collectively by all players. The team manager is only seen in peripherally. The victory is a team effort. Thus, Leadership overshadows the synergetic leader. A synergetic leader would not have it any other way. More of this will be discussed in chapter 8. So far, trust, integrity, and humility have been discussed. These attributes are directed towards team members. The next attribute is leader centric, competence.

Competence. Competence is necessary for a leader to operate efficiently and dynamically. Competence does not mean the leader is the expert on all facets of the overall organization. However, the leader must understand the organization as a whole *AND* (emphasis added) understand how the individual components of the organization interact synergistically to produce the stated goals. This interaction would include the relationship between the organization and the synergetic leader's teams led.

Regardless of any raw or inherent abilities of a leader, competence is comprised mostly of learned behaviors. These may be experienced by trial and error or be learned in formalized training. Training appropriate to the leadership role to be billeted must be accomplished with success. It does not benefit the organization, (or the stated goals) if a leader is competent in using Synergetic Leadership processes, but lacks competency in the tasks required for the stated goal achievement.

There are instances where the leader's competence is stressed. There may be changes in leader-led systems where no training was accomplished beforehand. In these cases, the leader uses one of two techniques, (or both simultaneously). First is to immediately begin appropriate training in the use and applicability of the new system. Secondly, the leader uses a subject expert as counsel when needing to use any part of the new system. However, there is a "catch" in this situation. What happens if the deficiency has to do with leadership competency in attributes or synergistic abilities?

The answer is simple but challenging to accept. The leader must find life skills training (formal counseling), where human interactive deficiencies can be discovered and addressed. Think of a new overseas manufacturing leader with little knowledge of the processes used and the cultural differences of the employees. This deficient leader may benefit from mentoring of peers and/or leadership supervisors alike. The key to this dilemma is to accept the fact there is a deficiency of the leader's competence. When this happens, the leader becomes less of a problem and part of the solution. Competence has also applicability to the next attribute, equanimity.

Equanimity (Steadfastness). The word equanimity is seldom used. It explains having composure in stressful situations. It is very comparable to being steadfast. The difference between the two is slight but important. A leader with equanimity displays a character of confidence by not letting irrational emotions take over a situation, be it either good or bad. Steadfastness applies more to the idea of not deviating from the expected behavior. If the leader is behaving with a steadfast attitude, then a deviation will not affect the expected direction of the team. A leader with equanimity may deviate from the initial direction but does so with complete composure. This composure asserts the leader has confidence in a solution at hand. It also asserts indirectly the leader's trust and confidence in the team led.

There is a relationship between competence and equanimity. The more competence displayed by the leader results in less negative consequences appearing when deviations to the stated goals occur. The leader does not dwell on the emotional effects of the problem and centers the effort towards the solution. In other words, "less drama equals more leadership" Another factor to enhance equanimity is logical, and this factor is the experience.

From a flight experience background, setting aside benefits of formal training, nothing is a better teacher than real-life experience itself. In aviation, the first time a pilot encounters an emergency is quite different than subsequent encounters. The first time the pilot encounters an actual emergency, the only tool for resolution is the training received. The subsequent scenarios allow the pilot to use both the technical training and similar experiences with the situation at hand. Experiencing a successful resolution of an emergency bodes well for equanimity on subsequent similar situations.

Furthermore, having equanimity in stressful situations allows the leader to be able to communicate and interact with team members to find a new solution to the presented problem. Having equanimity allows better interpersonal skills to happen since no intellectual energy is used in dealing with the emotional issues of the stressful situation. Therefore, having excellent interpersonal skills, our next attribute is a desirable synergetic leader's skill to aspire.

Interpersonal Skills/Communications. Communication skills vary greatly among leaders. The bad news is poor communication skills are detrimental to the practice of leadership, and especially in Synergetic Leadership. The leader must communicate the information in a way where the data is understood, and the stated goals related to the actions required are agreed to by the affected team members. Bluntly said, the team cannot achieve the stated goals unless the goal is understood completely, and the process to accomplish such a goal is agreed by all participants. This process requires a high level of communication skills.

The good news is that successful communication skills can be taught, honed, and improved. No matter how poor the leader is in communicating, there is great potential for improvement. In Synergetic Leadership, three steps are recommended. First, the leader must understand and admit there is a deficiency or failure to communicate with the team. Secondly, this deficiency must be presented to the team. The team can, and should, adjust their communicating skills with the leader as a means to achieve the stated goals. The team helps the synergetic process between the team and leader by ensuring bilateral responses and seeking clarification of the leader's information provided corresponding to the intended action. Thirdly, the leader must find formal training or mentoring partners and practice the required communication skills.

Regardless of the ability of the leader to communicate with the team, a crucial part of communication success is the communication loop. It is important to note the communication loop requires an acknowledgment of the communication received, and a mutual agreement of the stated message. Commonly, this is done by giving feedback. In

131

the case of a leader communicating data or actions, the leader should request feedback. Examples of these are open-ended **non-threatening** (emphasis added) questions such as "I might have given you too much data... Does this make sense to you?" or "This is what I see, what do you see?" or "Does your team understand what the new goal is?" The communication loop is advanced when the leader shows humble empathy with the data and/or actions presented, from the perspective of the receiver (team member). No matter which approach is used, communication does not occur until a response from the receiver is verified by the sender. In the case of leadership, the leader usually is the determinant in the closure of a proper communication loop. Speaking of communication, leaders should communicate with a positive mental attitude. This brings us to the next attribute.

Positive mental attitude. A common idiom, noted in Marines and ARMY military trench work, is as follows: "Misery loves company." The work in trenches can be extremely dangerous, in addition to being tedious. Furthermore, the situation can get much worse by logistical and environmental conditions (low ammunition, sporadic food, circadian rhythm disruptions, stress, and weather, etc.). On an interesting note, by synergetic analysis, even good can come out by two (or more) individuals being together, ... in misery. The empathy understood and shared produces a positive effect.

This can be accentuated with at least one individual having a positive mental attitude. The benefits of having a positive mental attitude are generally known. In Synergetic Leadership, this attitude is certainly a force multiplier. In other words, a group of individuals with a positive attitude will provide better results than the same number of individuals working with negative attitudes. There is something comforting in having a positive approach to situations. It is not a great revelation that tired, depressed, and oppressed individuals have problems developing solutions. Yet, an influx of positive data or attitudes can change any detrimental situation dramatically. This is done by asserting what can be done as opposed to what is not achieved. A good example of this is the case study in Chapter 7.

This is why it is important for Synergetic Leadership to address and accentuate the solution of the stated goals. This action is positive in nature. Even if the amount of possible solutions is minimal, just the participation aspect of synergetic effort produces a sense of movement towards the stated, and presumably better, situation.

A good example of morale improvement through active participation comes from the military. When in captivity, Prisoners of War (POWs) organize themselves into groups. Every effort is made by the captured military individuals to communicate and organize as groups. In fact, a whole hierarchy of sub-groups is contemplated and attempted. In this case, misery does love company, but the company serves for the betterment of the team members. Add a positive direction (mental attitude) of the efforts, and the result is much better than otherwise expected or achieved. Need an example, read chapter 7.

Positive mental attitude does not mean simply being funny. Humor does have a very positive effect on groups. If nothing else, the release of stress-reducing hormones from laughter is a positive effect. However, leaders may not have this characteristic in their social skills arsenal. It is to be equally beneficial to have a positive mental attitude without the need of extroversion or joviality. The positive mental attitude can be conveyed in written form, or in one on one conversations. The important element is the attitude, not the delivery system.

In regard to a non-jovial or introverted leader, one important concept needs to be mentioned. A synergetic leader should communicate the team members the expectation of non-extroverted demur from such a leader. People tend to accept introversion when it is openly discussed. Once this information is shared and accepted by the team members, the introverted synergetic leader can then focus on the stated goals. This focus will now be delivered with a positive mental attitude. The positive mental attitude will enhance the effort and participation of team members. Finally, the last desirable attribute to discuss has to do with any practical leadership, the "dreaded" organizational skills.

Organizational Aptitude (Management). When a large amount of data is saved in a computer, the efficient way to do so is to organize such data creating subsections (or files) inside the memory of the information systems. Leaders should do the same with the operational data and systems. Great leaders organize all their assets to better provide leadership results. In this section time, data, and future challenges are discussed as areas where organizational aptitude benefits a synergetic leader.

Time. There are volumes of books describing, applying and counseling on the need for time management and the negative effects of the misuse of time. There is no need to repeat or quote such data. There are common strategies for synergetic leaders with poor time management skills to address. The leader must admit the fact there is a deficiency in time management. If so, the leader must make an audit on how time is used to do all activities from wakeup to sleep (and add the amount of sleep). The time constriction (24 hours/day) and the time allotted for each known task must match. Activities are to be prioritized at the discretion of the leader. However, there are some things to consider.

There should be time to lead the stated goals of the team. If more is needed, the leader should delegate or reconsider the need for the specific task. The leader should have time for interpersonal relations, family and friends. These times should be known and allocated. If not, the leader may begin to deteriorate mentally. Life skill counselors spend much time deciphering and redirecting the efforts of those who begin to lose their interpersonal assets. Furthermore, time for oneself is equally important. Setting aside time to think through issues and expectations allows the leader to organize specific personal goals towards achievement.

A good synergetic leader with competent time organizational management skills probably understands the concept of task suspense. Even subordinates, who appreciate challenges, benefit from attainable and well-understood suspense for tasks. A good organizational leader, and in particular a synergetic leader, will describe when "things are due," and make the effort to have the individuals tasked to understand and accept the suspense for the action. The team member should comply with the agreed suspense. The leader should match the time required to complete the task including the time to allow for the leader's review. Depending on the task, a good synergetic leader request updates on the completion of the tasks to ensure compliance with the deadline.

Data. A competent synergetic leader must have systems that allow control of data in real-time. Most Information systems already comply with this basic principle. However, the leader should ensure the data on information systems is being used to the maximum of their potential. If not, time management is affected because the leader or subordinates

135

will be providing data that may already be available or could be derived from other available sources.

Future challenges. As important as the present time issues, suspense and data controls are for a leader, the direction of the future is equally important. Excellent organizational leaders are always thinking ahead of contemporaries. There should always be a sense of what future implications are compared to current activities. This is beneficial because the team members can define the effort produced for the current stated goals and simultaneously begin to think in terms of the future challenges ahead.

Summary. As simplistic as this chapter might appear, the practical application of Synergetic Leadership demands a leader to perform a personal self-audit of required leadership attributes. The synergetic leader should examine the success or deficiencies in the "things" which makes leaders succeed. Those items in which a leader succeeds are exploited. The items which need work should be addressed, and when deficient, be attenuated effectively. There is a constant challenge to be more organized and efficient. If approached correctly, the mere attempt to improve should provide better outcomes.

The information provided in this chapter buttresses nicely with the next chapter. Whereas in this chapter the attributes were discussed contextually, in the next chapter the concepts will be applied. Chapter 5 is more directive. This next chapter introduces the concepts of what to do, and what not to do, to achieve or ensure an excellent Synergetic Leadership environment.

Chapter 5

Synergetic Leadership "Do and Don'ts"

"Watch me, and do as I do" (Judges 7:17, ISV)

The biblical quote referenced above comes from the Bible's Old Testament. The story is detailed in chapters 6 through 8 in the book of Judges. It is the story of a very unlikely leader, Gideon. Why not take a break an read it now? It is well worth your time! In this story, God selects Gideon, a nonmilitary individual, to lead a small contingent of soldiers against a coalition army of 135,000 troops. By God's command, Gideon was given only 300 troops. To a gambler or actuary, the odds heavily favored the coalition. This strategic military engagement is similar to the famous battle of Thermopylae (in Greece, 480 B.C). In this battle, 300 Spartans kept at bay (for two days) an army of approximately 180,000 Persians using excellent military tactics. However, in the end, all 300 Spartans became casualties, most of them died.

In the case of Gideon, he and his troops completely succeeded. Yes, you read this right. Gideon's 300 troops were victorious against the 135,000-soldier strong Midianite army. Gideon's hastily conscripted, rag-tag miniature army defeated a large and superb coalition. Note that Gideon had God's grace and command. God's grace and influence is a force multiplier, as it was in this case. Setting aside the theological applications

137

and military lessons, it is important to note the last command Gideon gives to his troops before they enter the battle. His "do as I do" (Judges, 7:17 ISV) is the quintessential approach to excellent Synergetic Leadership. Gideon is an example of leading by doing the right thing, at the right time and for the right reason. This approach solidified and delivered the expected results. This notion of "doing the right thing" is the central theme of this chapter.

Listed in this chapter are critical actions (Do and Don'ts) an excellent synergetic leader delivers. These attributes may also apply to other leadership styles. Yet, these are mentioned as the foundation of critical elements for a leader, especially a synergetic leader, to aspire and team members to follow.

Also mentioned in this chapter are the behaviors which should be avoided. This avoidance helps ensure the cohesion developed by Synergetic Leadership. Whether the leader employs the "do" actions and/or avoids the "don't" actions, either effort should provide a better environment for the successful accomplishment of the stated goals.

Things to "Do".

1. Be "a" and/or "the", trusted agent. For a leader, being a trusted agent is of equal importance to competence and interpersonal skills. **The leader must be and act as a trusted agent.** This concept is true in most, if not all, leadership styles. Yet, in Synergetic Leadership, it is the most crucial aspect. Consensus is expected with each team member delivering the best result possible towards the stated goal. In this case, the team members must know whether good or bad results are delivered, the human aspect of the Synergetic Leadership exchange (between the leader and the individual team

members) is not affected. Thus, the trusted leader presents a human element of leadership which becomes a constant positive influence between the leader and the team members.

The synergetic leader is certainly expecting the best results. Yet, the leader understands the dynamics of imperfect people, working with imperfect systems, operating in an imperfect world. The synergetic leader empathizes with the team's challenges (whether group or individual) and employs whatever resources available to solve or attenuate these challenges. The trusted agent nature of the leader allows the team to concentrate on the stated goals. The leader supplies the team members with the resources necessary to achieve the stated goals using her/his competence of the required task. Therefore, competence is now discussed as a "Do" action.

2. *Deliver competence.* As discussed in Chapter 4, for a team to follow and assertively provide input, competence in the leader's skill set is required. However, a synergetic leader does not have to be the most competent resource. No leader has ever been the perfect model of any specific discipline or social competence. Yet, it goes without stating the idea of "If you do not know what you're doing, stop doing it!" If the leader does not understand a specific task, then the leader should either seek the proper training or find help with a team member who understands the competency required.

Normally leaders are selected for a leadership position by having a specific set of disciplinary and/or interpersonal skills. However, from the team members' perspective, it is a matter of showing the ability. Diplomas are great but showing that you have the competence to lead and simultaneously the technical skills for specific tasks is better. But in doing so, it is important to show deference, also known as respect.

3. *Show respect.* Respect delivers a very important ingredient in a Synergetic Leadership model. Respect from the leader brings communication and treatment of team members to the same level of the leader; regardless of age, status, gender, upbringing, cultural bias, or any human selective determinant. Respect makes the exchange of ideas between the sender and receiver equal. This is not to say that any or all exchange of ideas is selected for use. But at the least, discarded ideas from a team member do not affect the member's morale, because the leader accepted the input with respectful equitability. No human devaluation is perceived by either party. Since the leader can direct synergy and is the one to initiate or respond respectfully, then the synergetic aspect of the exchange remains intact. In the respectful exchange between leaders, or leaders with team members, it is very important the synergetic leader absorbs the input of team members with acute interest. This brings us to the next "Do" module, listening.

4. *Listen more than talk.* Depending on the leader's personality, listening can be a challenge. Active listening may be a deficient skill of either organizational team members or their leader. Yet it is an important aspect of being a trusted agent and showing respect. It is notable that great examples of leadership are enhanced or anchored with great communication, including listening, skills.

General Colin Powell has served not only as a military commander, but he also served as an American statesman. In his autobiography, he describes the center tenets of command. One of them involves listening. Paraphrasing the General's words as he is describing the interaction with troops, General Powell asserted the moment the troops do not tell you their problems is when they believe you don't care, or you are incompetent to help them. Then General Powell further asserted: "*Either one is a **failure** in leadership*" (author emphasis added). No better poignant analysis is required.

Notice General Powell talks about competency in solving the team member problems. This observation brings us to the next point, delivering on promises.

5. *Deliver on promises.* There is an inherent need to deliver on promises by the leader to the team members (or superiors). When a leader makes a promise to deliver a specific item, the leader must be sure the promise is, in fact, delivered. Delivering on promises strengthens the bond between a leader and team members. This is because the promise delivered matches the trust garnered by the team members. Also, the fulfillment of a promise accentuates competence and integrity. Competence is asserted because what was expected came to fruition. Integrity is asserted because the leader was the primary determinant for the delivery of the promise.

Failure to deliver on promises affects the trusted agent's attribute of a synergetic leader. If a leader cannot be trusted to deliver on promises, then what is the purpose of the direct engagement with the leader? Thus, it is imperative to deliver on promises. In the case of non-compliance (i.e. non-delivery of a promise), a good leader would explain the non-compliance to all individuals affected, with an explanation of the facts for the non-compliance. Furthermore, the leader should emphasize empathy for non-delivery of what was expected. The general thought should center on the ***effect*** of the non-delivery, and not the non-delivery itself. In other words, the leader would show empathy with the direct result of the effect of non-delivery to the affected parties.

It is understandable for things to not go right sometimes. In addition to the negative effects of promises non-delivery, there can be issues with interpersonal dynamics between team members. This undesirable anomaly leads us to the next assertive "Do". This module is related to consensus.

6. *Seek consensus vital to the expected goal, even at the expense of some team's inner "click" dynamics.* In Synergetic Leadership, the process of obtaining the expected goal centers on the team's efforts. Consider Synergetic Leadership is not leader centric. Neither is Synergetic Leadership a specific team member-centric. The Synergetic Leadership system is both goal-oriented and *team* (author emphasis added) centric. Therefore, the consensus solution and delivery of the stated goals take primacy over individuals (including the leader) and sections of team members within the organization.

At times, this leads to friction among members of the organization. Some "clicks," or subsections of teams, may find themselves being overwritten by the need for cohesion to execute the desired goal. It is important to note these sub-teams are counter-indicated to the object of Synergetic Leadership. To solve this dilemma, the synergetic leader must address the possibly antagonistic "pseudo-leader," and this individual's followers, the need to follow synergetic practices within the organization. The concept is simple enough: It is about what's right, not about who's right. There is a way to address this dilemma in Synergetic Leadership. To address the friction produced by inner teams, many questions need to be asked by the leader relating to the team's cohesiveness. The leader must find the best answers, which leads us to our next point.

7. *Ask direct questions, accept direct answers and then seek explanations.* A general principle of legal proceedings is for an attorney never to ask a question to which the answer is not already understood, and complementary to the attorney's goal. Such is not the case with Synergetic Leadership. Generally, the use of leadership is a quest to arrive at a better solution than the one where no leadership is exercised. Therefore, discovery is part of the process. What's discovered may, or may not be, what is expected. It is the duty of the leader to deal with the issue and resolve the matter.

The best way to achieve this resolution is to disengage any notional or emotional filters to a discussion and accept what may come as a result. A leader should ask direct, even uncomfortable, questions. For example, "Why does this decision upset you? "or, "What other options can you offer for a better outcome?". Team members should provide unfiltered inputs, especially if the leader is truly a trusted agent. The answers may direct the leader and team members towards the solution. This solution may be unexpected.

In order to accomplish this resolution, the leader needs to follow the "Do" #4 "Listen more than talk." When a question from the leader is answered, the leader should consider analyzing the answer in three ways.

First, the answer should define the "what?" The answer should give data for the pursue of the stated goal. However, communication is not a sterile construct. The personal bias from the sender and/or deliverer is infused in the answer. The answer may include unnecessary data, worse yet, appropriate related data may be withheld. This phenomenon brings us to the next part of the analysis.

Secondly, the answer should represent the "how?" This "how" is the personal side of the answer given. The author of the answer is trying to lead the questioner to a solution, or the author's idea of what needs to be done. This answer may be done in the best interest of the team, in the best interest of the author, or perhaps both. A true leader and trusted agent can dissect the personal proclivities of answers by knowing the perspective of the author's answer. The more a team member announces any bias of the answer, the better the chance the

143

solution to be organically beneficial. This happens because when an individual bias is uncovered, the perspective of a proposal is better understood from the team member's point of view. This point of view brings us to the final analysis.

Lastly, the answer should clearly identify the "Why?" In other words, the given answer needs to explain its primacy or mutual exclusivity against all other possible answers. If it does, and the team can accept the answer, then success is most likely to result. The "why" is the third step of answer analysis, because the leader must first know the data (what) and then the bias (how) before the selection (why) is used. If after due diligence, the answer proves to be ineffective, then consider the next "Do" action.

8. *Have a back-up plan.* Never, never, ever proceed without an alternative plan or an exit strategy. Failure to not having a back-up plan may lead to an unrecoverable situation. This is where understanding the issue and asking the appropriate questions are keys to Synergetic Leadership success.

It is hard to fathom a leadership decision or action where there is no backup plan, at least notionally. Whether actual or notionally, the leader must announce whatever consequences to all team members before the action are to be taken. If the back-up/exit strategy is notional, announce to the team members as such. Knowing the reality of the situation, even if a bad outcome is possible, allows each team member to process the truth. The next "Do" involves the continuity of leadership, the need for future success.

9. *Mentor leadership, the leader (you) will be replaced.*
"Father Time" waits for no one. All leaders are replaced. The tenure of the leadership role is tenuous and time-limited. In the Air Force, a command assignment is usually no longer than two years. Therefore, find the "up and coming" leaders and mentor these individuals' synergetic abilities.

It is amazing to witness organizations where no mentorship occurs, and an "heir apparent" is not even considered. In the military, business environment and team sports, the "next individual up" is usually known. This is true in good leadership. However, leadership and especially Synergetic Leadership needs to be mentored. Leadership skills should not be acquired by osmosis or emulation. Leadership skills are honed by mentoring. This takes time and effort. Both are rewarded when the "next in line" take the organization forward. A good synergetic leader, like a good parent, would also hope and expect the mentored to exceed the performance of their mentor.

If you are indeed an effective (or whatever accolade you feel is appropriate) leader, regardless of which style of leadership used, you should "clone" yourself by mentoring. It is part of the legacy of great leadership (more on this in Chapter 8). The leader owes the mentorship of the heirs apparent for the success in the continuum of the organization.

This leads to the next four points of this chapter. These points are the "ultimate Dos". These goals encompass the center of Synergetic Leadership's expected achievements. These are a summary of the ultimate goals of the synergetic leader.

10. Goal #1, *Deliver a standard, not just exercise authority*. Authority exercises control, leadership delivers standards. The two concepts are not mutually exclusive. The difference is the impetus. Authority is about ensuring the directive figure (leader) influences the followers (team) in a specific, and exclusive, direction. One of the goals of leadership, and in particular Synergetic Leadership, is to emphasize the standard to be achieved. In this case, the authority used is only as needed to deliver the stated goals.

The need for power over the team and its' resources are only applied as needed to deliver the stated goals. Any further use is just a quest for unilateral power from the leader. The latter occurs when the leader only operates in one known leadership style. This style is authoritative in nature. If not for the lack of the understanding of other leadership styles, then unwarranted authority is exercised as a selfish or self-centered attitude. Good leaders always focus on the stated goals and the team which will achieve such results.

11. Goal #2, *Deliver a caring attitude.* Caring for the team is more than an attribute, it is an attitude. In doing so, the leader gives the team a reason to believe in the leadership and themselves. This goal is manifested in various ways. A caring attitude demonstrates a tenet of the leader being a trusted agent. A sincere caring attitude tells the team members, both individually and as a group, the leader has the best interest of team members in mind. This tends to center the team around the leadership provided. Thus, a caring attitude fosters a trusting attitude from the team members.

Furthermore, a leader's caring attitude toward team members may foster the same attitude among the team members themselves. Caring attitudes are a positive direction and usually emulated if fostered. (Positive attitudes are discussed further in Chapter 8). If not emulated by example, leaders may direct this demeanor as an expected mode of participation in the team. However, the latter is easier accomplished when the leader delivers a caring attitude.

12. Goal #3, *Understand the difference between wisdom and intelligence.* Leadership benefits from the goal of understanding the difference between wisdom and intelligence. There is a specific difference between the two concepts. Wisdom is applied intelligence. Intelligence relates to Who, What, Where, When and How. Wisdom is related to why.

Leaders will work with a vast array of intelligent individuals. These individuals may want to contribute their intelligence to the tasks at hand. However, the knowledge of the data or process may not coincide with the applicability of such knowledge. In other words, the intelligent answer may be at hand, but for a variety of reasons, it may not be used or may be modified from the original input. Leaders consider the solution as a construct to affect not only the stated goals but the implications to other systems affected by the course of action taken. To understand trans-organizational implications, experience and wisdom are both required. It is the purview of the leader, in particular, a leader using synergy, to glean the appropriate construct of the stated goals via intelligence and wisdom congruently.

13. Goal #4, *Leave the institution better than you found it*. The ultimate goal, and a good measure of the leader's success and effectiveness, is the concept of perpetual improvement. All leaders should leave the team in a better position than when initially led. In theory, subsequent leaders will eventually arrive at a perfect team construct. However, there is no historical precedent of this happening. This may be due because change is a known constant part of the human experience continuum. Thus, today's leadership stated goals may not be tomorrow's priority. Worse yet, today's stated goals may become tomorrow's challenge. The good news is the changing continuum allows for new leadership opportunities. Synergetic Leadership flourishes where applicability and opportunity present themselves. In this vein, it is important to avoid pitfalls that are contrary to a synergistically led environment. Thus, it is time to discuss the antithesis of "Dos", better known as "Do nots".

Things _NOT_ to "Do" (Don'ts).

1. _Don't accept failure in attitude._ Poor performance can be accepted as it pertains to failure of training, system applications, or lack of particular resources. All these can be remediated. Nonacceptance is an attitude problem. Although attitude problems can be remediated, there is an important distinction. Systematic failures normally are the result of poor performance not allowing success. The attitude was positive, but the result was not.

An attitude problem is the team members decision not to direct a positive outcome. In this case, success could have been achieved, but there was an unconscious or lackadaisical attitude that precluded success. This is a poor operational approach, but it can be worse. Unfortunately, there is a possibility the poor attitude is intentional. This would be the worst-case scenario.

Lack of appropriate positive attitude must be identified, administered, and resolved with utmost expediency. The solution may be drastic. The solution may include team member dismissal. This is not due exclusively to the detrimental result, but unfortunately, inappropriate attitudes are contagious. This is further mentioned in Chapter 8. The resolution of the inappropriate behaviors buttresses the next "do not" concept, delaying bad news.

2. _Don't delay bad news_. Some leaders believe in delaying bad news. Most team members are sensitive enough to notice clues of impending bad news. Although a synergetic leader may have to wait until all data is available to deliver the onerous news, the leader must not delay its' delivery.

The trusted agent tenet comes in play at these moments. Bad news does not improve over time, _unless_ it may

change for the better, depending on future events. In this case, a good synergetic leader will explain all the information at hand and brief all team members as soon as all data is confirmed. This brief should be done in as personal a forum as possible. Empathy with the effect of the bad news on the team member will be paramount. The synergetic leader may exacerbate bad news by attempting to attenuate the effects of bad news. This brings us to the next "Don't," the mutually exclusive solution to problems.

3. *Don't accept being part of the problem, be part of the solution (for both the leader and team members).* By definition, leadership is about solving challenges to achieve success. The leader deals with both problems, and its antonym, solutions. In a theoretical construct, the problems are opposing forces to success. The leader focusses on the solution at the expense of the effects of the problem. Therefore, the impetus requires the synergetic leader and the team members to address solutions together. Not addressing the solution becomes part of the problem, or the problem itself. The leader must always focus the team members on solutions. The problem is just the starting point of the task ahead. Focusing on the solution should lead to a synergetic answer.

Unfortunately, sometimes the synergetic answer makes the team realize the problem is within the team itself. This notion takes the team to a less than optimal realization. The problem is then within the team dynamics. As such, the next "Don't" become a leader's priority.

4. As a leader, *don't assume everything is copacetic, not everything is "O.K".* You may have heard the idiom: "Call the baby ugly when it is." This applies to Synergetic Leadership. You will reprimand and/or take administrative actions to include the dismissal (firing) of a team member. Do not berate

149

the individual's persona. It's about behavior and/or unmet expectation. You can believe in the team member, it's up to this individual to change their attitude and/or direction. Showing assertive disapproval and disappointment at the **BEHAVIOR**, and not the individual, is not a bad thing. Sometimes, a "one-way" conversation may be the catalyst for change. A good synergetic leader will end the discourse exemplifying the potential of the individual, and contrast with the demonstrated deficiency (example: *you are better, and can do better, than this*). The synergetic leader may change the attitude to the betterment of the individual and the team. If not, the conversation may help the individual achieve success in a new and different organizational opportunity. It may be a time to make a change. Speaking of time, the next two "Don't" addresses an ever-enveloping leadership challenge, time management.

5. *Don't give a vague deadline. Whenever possible, give a generous but firm deadline (for specific tasks).* Time management for task completion tends to follow the lowest common denominator of efficiency. Thus, work completion tends to occupy the time given for the task. This may, or may not be, the most efficient use of time. Here is where technical competence and leadership competence intersect. A competent leader should understand the complexity of a task and the abilities of the team members to complete the task. Using these two data points, the leader assigns a deadline. This deadline is normally earlier than the required deadline expected from the leader, i.e. the aforementioned, "Have a back-up plan." In other words, whenever possible, the deadline should allow the leader time to react to unexpected issues. The use of time by the team member should be more efficient than just giving the task alone and allow the team member to manage their time constraints. Speaking of time, the next "Do not" also applies to the time continuum.

6. *Do not waste time, work efficiently and qualitatively, not quantitatively.* This notion is common in any realm of our lives. The problem is the lack of specificity. A good leader approaches time management with great emphasis on specific time management-related goals. A good starting point is this: If a leader spends more than 50 hours a week in direct work-related activities, then the leader may be incompetent, have an understaffed team, or is working inefficiently (perhaps a combination of the three). Time management and/or systems solutions trump inefficiency, training trumps incompetence. A leader, and in particular a synergetic leader, has direct control of both efficiency and competence. A leader will seek solutions in either non-delivered expectations. Understaffing can be directly controlled by adding human resource assets. A leader advocates assertively the need for appropriate staff levels to higher management echelons.

This brings us to the problem of not being able to immediately solve the inefficiency. If so, the leader must explain the inefficiency, as detailed as possible, and present it to the team for synergetic consideration. Inefficiencies contribute to wasteful time usage. It is important to note long hours of continuous effort is not sustainable, and will negatively affect the leader, the team, and the stated goals. The last "Don't" to be presented delivers the center theme of the "Do's and Don'ts," it relates to a leader's focus.

7. *Do not focus on being a great leader, focus on exercising great leadership skills.* Too many individuals practicing leadership focus on the optics (read themselves), and not on the actual process. True greatness in leadership comes as a result of the leadership skills developed and utilized. The moniker of a leader may be simply awarded, but it is truly earned. Leaders may have to make unilateral decisions when no other synergetic derived outcomes are available, and/or time is critical. Synergetic Leadership can be restricted by many factors. Yet most of the time, Synergetic Leadership is available and warranted to achieve the stated goals of the team. The use of the leadership construct which achieves success is to be the main impetus of a leader. Whoever the actual leader is quasi-superfluous when compared to the leadership style used. Accentuating a leader is usually associated with egocentric bravado or synergetic incompetence. Accentuating the leadership outcomes exemplifies the result of the team.

Summary. The "Dos and Don'ts" presented in this chapter serves as a tool to delineate actions commensurate with Synergetic Leadership. There are specific actions to enhance the use of synergy in a leadership construct. The leader must understand and employ the "Do" modules. Simultaneously, synergy is enhanced by the emphasis of the "Don'ts". Both actions should solidify the leadership environment towards the achievement of the stated goals.

Chapter 6
Synergetic Leadership, a Balance Dilemma

"If the world were perfect, it wouldn't be" Yogi Berra

Yogi Berra's idiom poses the simple axiom: an imperfect world is normal. To Yogi, an unbalanced world is normal. This is similar to the dichotomy of resources in Synergetic Leadership. This chapter attempts to describe the notion of Synergetic Leadership being a balance of the use of resources to produce a better outcome. It is possible to explain to a granular level the intricacies of the balance required for a prosperous, or perhaps perfect, Synergetic Leadership environment. However, one of the purposes of this book is to give you a clear, and hopefully simple way, to apply Synergetic Leadership in a practical manner.

Using the synergetic leader definition as a model, it should be easy to understand what forces need to be in balance for the successful use of Synergetic Leadership. The definition of Synergetic Leadership is essentially a cause-effect association. Recall the Input-Process-Output flow presented in Chapter 1. It is almost akin to a mathematical equation. With this in mind, in this chapter, the concept will be examined backward. The definition of leadership is based on three simple words, **Human Applied Synergy**. Thus, the stated goal in this

153

axiom is to achieve synergy. One side of the synergetic equation (the outcome or result) is synergy.

If the result of the equation is synergy, then the other side of the equation is the effort applied by humans (the input and process). These ideas can generate all kinds of questions. Here are a few, and these will be addressed individually.

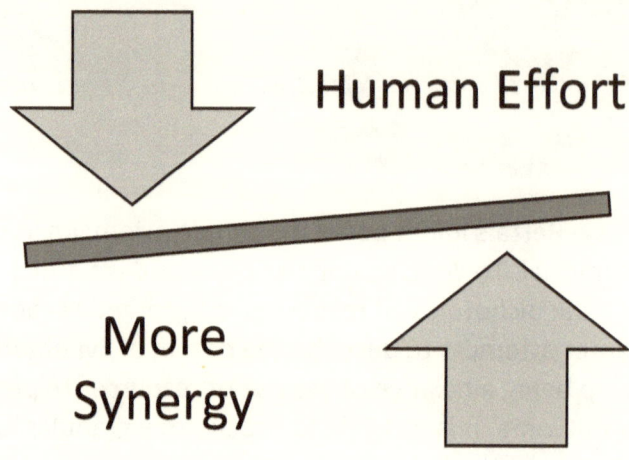

If you apply more human effort, do you get more synergy? Maybe, maybe not. If more synergy is defined as a more diverse set of solutions to the stated goal, the arithmetic of synergy will produce a better result. This is to say having more people trying to solve a challenge (using synergy) should deliver more ideas for a solution. Thus, adding more individuals to the issues will, in fact, produce more results. But more is not the same as arguing for better results. The proper application of synergy results in the stated goals. In order to achieve the stated goals, the latter has to be clearly defined and understood by all participants. Of the Synergetic Leadership participants, the synergetic leader takes responsibility of understanding, because if the leader does not understand the stated goals, then it would be difficult or even impossible for the leader to advocate a solution for the challenge and apply proper resources. Therefore, if the leader understands the issue and applies the right synergy, then more human effort (more people) will result in more synergy, quantitively.

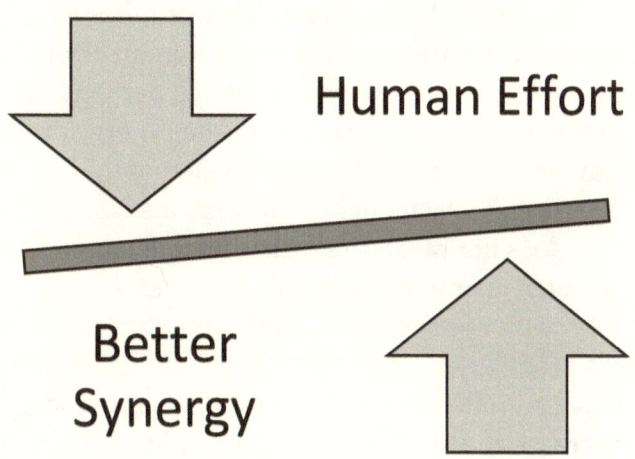

If you apply more human effort, do you get better synergy? This question leads to a better answer to the previous construct of balancing the Synergetic Leadership equation. The answer is it should. It is natural to assume that the more "heads" you insert into the problem, the better chance to come to a better outcome or solution to a problem. In essence, a better outcome by cooperative efforts defines synergy. So, more people should result in better synergy. However, what is "more human effort?" Is the question of assuming more human resources with the same level of effort or more effort from the same amount of personnel involved? This leads to the question of what amount of human effort is required for success. Most chefs are familiar with the idiom "Too many cooks (or chefs) spoils the soup." This principle applies to Synergetic Leadership. The secret is to find the right amount of human resources to provide the correct amount of input to the stated goal, and then have these individuals cooperate to achieve synergy. Therefore, more human resources normally should mean better synergy also. This is because the cooperative nature of synergy is enhanced when more human resources are exercised.

If you change the synergy required (less), does this minimize the need or use of the human effort? The answer to this question is mostly ambivalent... perhaps. Changing the side of the equation which refers to the synergy expected could change the need for the human element, but it may not. The stated goal which requires synergy may, and often do change. This does not mean the team members need to be reduced or changed in any way. But unless the tasked team members are otherwise needed, or could be used in other areas, why change the team's synergetic effort applied? Today's less tasked team may be tomorrow's crisis center. So, less synergy required may decrease the amount of human application needed, but such reduction may not be wise to employ.

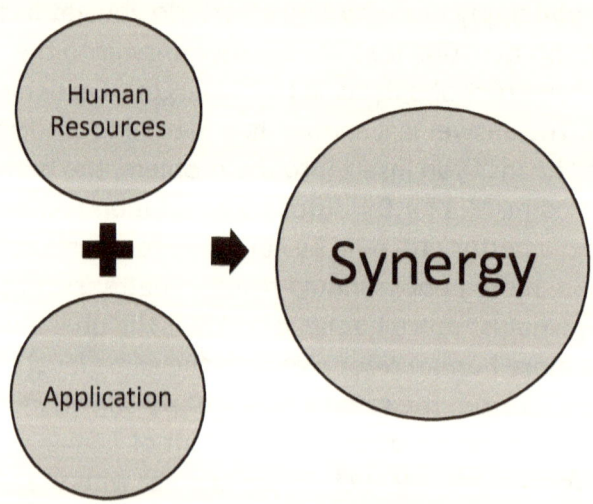

How do the stated goals stabilize the equation? The stated goals stabilize the equation by determining how much synergy is required to achieve such goals. This amount may be known to the assembled team, or not known (i.e., a challenge not seen or worked on before by the group). Either way, it is the stated goals that determine what amount, and perhaps which human element, will be required to achieve such goals. The human element will be codified and enumerated by the applicability of skills. In other words, if two or three individuals understand the problem, then these may be enough to achieve the synergy required to reach the stated goals. If the challenge is more complex, or at a much grander scale, it may be necessary to find additional human resources to bear against the challenge. As it has been stated before, the more synergetic answers, the more people are needed. Otherwise, the smaller group of participants must understand multiple synergetic challenges, simultaneously. The latter may not be possible. The bottom line is the stated goal stabilizes the synergy equation by determining the number of human resources to be applied to the challenge.

What does all this mean to a practitioner of synergetic leadership? The one-word answer is simple, balance. However, the achievement of this balance is much more complex. A synergetic leader needs to understand the issue or stated goal *and simultaneously* know which human assets to assign to achieve the synergetic solution. The secret of how to achieve this balance lies within the attributes of a synergetic leader, and in particular, competence.

Thus, if the application of leadership styles, and in particular synergetic leadership, is required for the success of the stated goals of the operations, then an acute

157

understanding of the competence required for the use of synergy is required. This, in turn, requires strong synergetic attributes of the synergetic leader, in particular, competence (See chapter 4). The synergetic leader must balance the stated goal with the human element to produces the synergetic answer to the challenge. The right application of this balance would under normal circumstances produce success, or at the least, a better outcome than if no synergetic approach was attempted.

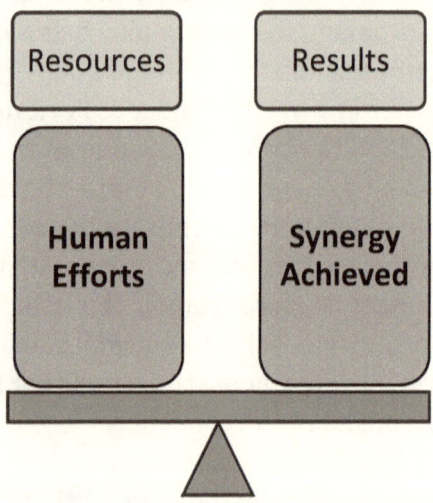

One last comment on this subject is appropriate, and it has to do with control. The practitioner of synergetic leadership must understand the control aspect of the two sides of the synergetic leadership equation. Controlling the human element is the basis of the concept of leadership. The leader controls the human effort to achieve the stated goals. The methodology is synergy. The leader also controls the amount of synergy attempted because the solutions presented are usually the prerogative of the leader to use, or not use. It is also the synergetic leader's prerogative to accept, or discard, the myriad of possible solutions for consideration. Normally, the solution is adopted by the leader, but not always. This is done for a variety of reasons, none of which are compatible with Synergetic Leadership. It is paramount the synergetic leader understands the proper use of the control authorized by the leader's hierarchy will have a direct effect on the use and results of the team's synergy. In fact, control of the synergetic approach towards the stated goals will result in success or failure. A synergetic leader chooses wisely.

Summary. The expected results of Synergetic Leadership require a balance of human resources and the effort expended, i.e. synergy. By adding more human resources, more synergy may be achieved. However, synergy may also be improved by more participation of the same number of team members. The balancing component is the match of the right amount of human resources applying the right amount of synergy to produce the stated goals. The synergetic leader balances the human effort and the synergy required to achieve the stated goal. This balance ensures the right amount of synergy is derived by the right amount and effort of human resources.

Chapter 7

Synergetic Case Study: Shamrock Flight

"Quis Custodiet Ipsos Custodes" Juvenal, Satires VI

The teaser of this chapter is written by the Roman satirical writer, Juvenal. It translates to "who will guard the guards." Originally, writing with a satirical purpose, Juvenal was trying to give context to the problem of control in interpersonal relations. Yet, in more general terms, this passage shows the distorted importance between the service provider (the guards), and the need for these providers to be served. If the guards were doing their respective jobs, (taking care of the safety and security of their respective posts), then who was taking care of them? Was taking care of the guards themselves as important as the guards taking care of their posts? And if so, which responsible party is the guardian of the guards?

In general terms, the leader is responsible to employ all available resources to ensure the best results by team members towards the stated goals. Perhaps the simple answer to Juvenal's question was this: the higher echelon leader was (or should be) the guardian of the guards.

A general axiom of this book is the use of a Synergetic Leadership construct to make the leader be a "Custodiet Custodes" (guardian of the guards). Team members require the necessary resources to achieve the success of the stated goals.

Practical Leadership: Making the Case for Synergy

When the leader provides the resources, the team member employs the resources along with their own assets and attributes to reach the stated goals of the organization. Therefore, in theory, Juvenal's guardian of the guards is the leader of the aforementioned guards. The construct is theoretical, of course. It could be argued the guardian of the guards is not the designated leader of a group. Guards could be guarded by external sources other than the designated leader, or a pseudo-leader (non-formally designated), or perhaps a colleague. But the premise of the question is the designation of the guardian of the guards, and the importance of this individual or individuals. If the assumption is the designated leader is the guardian of the guards, then an ominous question is presented. What happens when the guardian of the guards is dysfunctional or destructive towards the guards, or the stated goals, or both?

This brings us to the case of the Shamrock flight. This case study will demonstrate what can happen when the formally designated leader operates in a dysfunctional and anti-synergetic environment. In this setting, the team begins to deteriorate towards inefficacy and collapse. Under these conditions, the stated goals may not be achieved. In this particular case, the employment of the "guardian of the guards" had to be modified to redirect the team towards success. Synergy was a vital part of the solution to the team's issues.

Thus, the case study of the Shamrock Flight is a story of applying synergy to combat a distorted stated goal emphasis. The best summary of this leadership case is the concept of synergy overcoming a vacuum of leadership skills by a designated leader, and the re-emergence of a team-centered approach to success. This is their story.

Because this story uses military acronyms not readily familiar to most readers, a moniker for the three primary individuals will be used to facilitate the readability and understanding of the story.

The dysfunctional formal Director of Operations (DO) and new Commanding Officer (CC), will be referred to as **FIST**.

The new Director of Operations (DO) will be referred to as **Quixote**.

The Assistant Director of Operations (ADO) will be referred to as **Abodekeeper**.

And, without further ado...

The Shamrock Flight was a small United States Air Force unit flying airlift support missions. In the Spring of 1999, due to unusual circumstances, the designated commander (CC) was relieved from command (fired). The designated heir apparent, the current Director of Operations or DO (FIST) was elevated to the CC position. A new DO (Quixote) was procured using standard personnel acquisition protocols. Quixote would arrive approximately 90 days from the existing DO-to-CC leadership succession. FIST became the new commander.

For FIST, the elevation to a leadership position from the current DO to CC would be a normal progression for an existing DO. This move to a new CC position is realized by a vacancy fill, or as in this case, loss of a CC in the DO's unit. Yet, designating a new leader and having a positive leadership environment is not necessarily symbiotic. Sometimes, they are mutually exclusive. This was the case in this scenario.

FIST was ill-suited for command. Although this individuals' technical competency (flying) was well above average, leadership and interpersonal skills were not the forte of his leadership attributes. FIST displayed a borderline passive/aggressive personality, a despotic demeanor that inspired fear and resentment from the officer and enlisted members assigned. His personal agenda involved getting promoted to a very specific position at the current base of the assignment. To achieve this goal was very challenging, as there was only one available position of its' kind at this operating base. In order to achieve this very specific and exclusive desire, FIST contrived two specific goals. The first was to produce overwhelmingly excellent results at any price. The second was to act as if the processes and actions of the unit were comparable and/or almost identical to the prospective gaining billet of the higher echelon command (the aspired position). FIST reasoned his command would demonstrate excellence in delivering the current stated goals while simultaneously achieving the expectations of the aspired billet.

FIST's command was characterized by a desire to impress the prospective hiring authority (at the base). At the same time, every effort to avoid even the perception of failure with the current higher echelon was exercised. Any expense toward these two goals was accepted in a Machiavellian approach to leadership. Synergy with the subordinates and the synergy of the subordinates with each other were of no concern to this leader. FIST exercised an authoritarian leadership style where such style was unnecessary and counterproductive. Within months of FIST's assumption of command, this unit became dangerously dysfunctional.

Examples of this dysfunctional leadership theater abounded. FIST had a desire to use regulatory compliance to override any improvement needed to enhance productivity. In other words, if a synergetic solution was not implicitly directed by governing regulations, the idea was immediately discarded. Conflicts in regulatory compliance between different command

163

directives were met with an attempt to dual compliance of both regulations simultaneously, even if contradictory.

For example, two separate and different formatted flight schedules were published daily. One (the official schedule) was to be used for the unit's higher echelon compliance, and the other for the informational use of the operating base. The schedules had the same information but FIST insisted to cater the informational schedule to the accepted format at the operating base. This was not necessary. Thus, the flight schedulers were manually compiling a plethora of information and presenting this information in different formats. This led to multiple typographical mistakes between the two different schedules. FIST would compare both schedules and note every mistake with surgical precision. This produced an environment where morale was decimated, every day the schedulers could count on being reprimanded for lack of this artificial compliance. [The solution was very simple. The official schedule's format could be taught in minutes to the receiver of this document at the operating base, and have them translate the data accordingly to their needs. This was accomplished day #2 after FIST left the unit] These types of nonsensical prerogatives frustrated the unit's cohesiveness.

The unit's morale plummeted. The response by the team was abysmal, and the attitude of team members began to erode towards self-destruction. The lower-ranking officers began considering failing an upcoming formal military inspection **on purpose**, in hopes FIST would get fired. This would be tantamount to the idiom "getting rid of the baby with the bathwater." To stop this behavior, one member of the officer corps reminded the bellicose team members that, again the idiomatic, "we will sink with the ship", and the soon newly arrived DO, Quixote, (and new heir apparent) may be fired also. This individual attempting to stop the self-destructive behavior was the unit's ADO (Assistant Operations Officer, third in the hierarchy of command), you shall meet him later in this story. His moniker is Abodekeeper.

One member was so distraught, he went home one day and began to cry to his wife in complete despair. This was not a weak-minded individual with a deficient level of coping skills. This individual was a fine military officer with documented laudatory evaluations. He was also a good aviator and a trusted agent. He was trusted to fly high ranking officers into potentially hazardous environments. His despair was related to not having a peer or trusted agent in the organization, in this vacuum of counter-synergetic leadership, to share concerns. He turned to his only trusted agent and closest ally, his spouse. There he found an avenue to release his frustration which was consuming him. This individual was a fine aviating officer, who saw very little future as an officer and/or pilot, in this desert of despair.

Another and perhaps worse example followed. Upon the arrival of Quixote, this new team member was quickly exposed to the ongoing disintegration of any type of healthy Synergetic Leadership construct within this unit. The tipping point for the need for action came within weeks of the new Quixote's arrival. One morning, a mid-grade officer came to the Quixote and asked to meet in private at his office. The request was immediately granted.

This officer had 6 years remaining on his service retainability (active duty service commitment) with the Air Force. This meant he could not voluntarily leave the Air Force unless the Air Force separated him for cause (until his commitment was served). This individual asked Quixote what he would have to do to get released or get some relief from his present active duty commitment. The reason he wanted to leave was the present toxic environment. Trying to diffuse the

165

situation with a little humor, Quixote said it would take him running naked in front of the Wing Commander (a General Officer), in the middle of a staff meeting, to get kicked out of the Air Force. To his horror, Quixote saw this officer looking directly at him as if contemplating when the next staff meeting would be convened. Obviously, something had to be done, immediately.

The issue was straightforward. The remaining higher-ranking members of the unit (other than FIST) must now deflect the despotic behavior, improve morale, and mentor the junior officers to succeed through this adversarial and unsynergetic environment. This approach would have to last until the present commander's tenure was completed. Quixote was a grade lower than FIST, thus not at par with the FIST's authority. So, it would take more than Quixote's effort to rectify the current condition. At this moment, a new leadership construct came into play. Synergetic Leadership would be attempted. However, this synergetic effort would have to be attempted in subterfuge.

Applied synergetic process. A meeting between the Quixote and Abodekeeper was convened. For two hours, a myriad of ideas, processes, and alternatives was contrived. In the end, the decision was clear on what to do. Quixote and Abodekeeper would attempt to both attenuate FIST's despotic leadership style and congruently lead the unit in subterfuge. This meant until a new change of command happened, Quixote's primary duty was to attempt deflection of all negative orders, counterproductive ideas or protocols from the commander. Quixote would act as a buffer between FIST and the team members. In such a role, Quixote would attempt to dissuade the despotic behaviors from the commander. This was to be Quixote's full-time, and perhaps his most important, task. Therefore, Abodekeeper would now assume a "de facto" role of both DO (Quixote's designated role) and act in some respects as FIST. These two individuals would attempt to lead synergistically in subterfuge.

This use of synergy was human resource-centric. Abodekeeper became a key player, even though he was one grade lower than Quixote. Abodekeeper had a unique ability to light up the room with humor and antics. He was also a very competent aviator, extremely intelligent and interpersonally adept. Because of the despotic behavior of the commander, prior to Quixote arriving, this individual was the center of what little morale was left in the unit. Abodekeeper will now play a key role in the development of a plan to reverse course and counter the current leadership vacuum.

Synergetic outcome. Quixote's success in abating the onslaught of despotism and morale deflating interactions (from FIST) with the subordinates was met with partial or mixed results. Due to the Quixote's lesser rank, and FIST's inability to understand or accept the inputs from Quixote, the effectiveness to deflect FIST's detrimental behavior was mixed. The effort helped a little with the general environment, but not as much as it was hoped. However, one good outcome of this part of the effort appeared. The unit began to notice the effort from both Quixote and Abodekeeper. To quote the previously noted idiom, "misery loves company" became a reality. The team could see the interactions of Quixote and Abodekeeper as part of a plan to alleviate the units' environmental toxicity. Quixote and Abodekeeper were trying diligently to create a positive and synergetic environment.

Abodekeeper enjoyed a much better outcome. This individual became, in short order, the rallying point for the unit. This individual became part Commander, part Director of Operations, part cheerleader, part discipline enforcer, part counselor, part mentor, part judge, part comrade, and full-time

167

morale officer. Positive results were immediately achieved. The cadre (team) began to trust and engage with these superiors. The team began to trust in this leadership model. The team began to believe in the stated goals and put forth a synergetic effort towards a new direction.

The results were amazing. In less than 9 months, the unit was awarded Unit of the Quarter and Unit of the Year accolades by the higher commanding echelon. Members were inspired to participate and work together despite the constant harsh and toxic environment. They used the best of themselves to make, again another idiom, "lemonade out of lemons." The unit became a resounding success. As FIST departed (to the aspired position at the base), Quixote became the commander, and the expected normal leadership military environment returned. The unit maintained its new Synergetic Leadership construct.

The Shamrock Flight case illustrates what can be possible if leadership becomes a priority somewhere in the organization, not necessarily at the top. Synergy does not necessarily come from the top, or even near the top of the hierarchy. In this case, it came from a lesser hierarchical leader, and a pseudo assigned leader. It is interesting to note the later (Abodekeeper) was more successful than the former (Quixote). The recognition of the unit's performance (by the higher echelons) was the result of a successful synergetic environment. In this case, synergetic leadership processes and protocols were shared to produce the desired outcome. Synergy can be attained even in negative centered environments. When properly applied, synergy can produce success. In the case of the Shamrock Flight, it was synergy that delivered and exceeded the stated goals.

Chapter 8

Synergetic Leadership Zingers

"Hey batter batter, swing batter batter!"

(Common baseball batter banter)

If you ever played Little League baseball, you might remember the banter from defensive team players to the opposing team's batter at home plate. "Hey batter batter, swing batter batter!" was designed by defenses to try to confuse or "spook" the batter to swing early and strikeout. Even in Major League Baseball, you might hear kids in the stands repeating this banter to the pros at home plate. This banter sort of "sticks" to you for the rest of your life. You remember it for as long as baseball is enjoyed. The same is true in the use of zingers.

The best way to apply the general concepts of this book is to give you a set of zingers that encompass the general guidance of this book. A zinger is an impact phrase or statement. In this case, the "zingers" are related to synergetic centered leadership. These notions are designed to stick with the leader exercising a practical application of leadership, especially Synergetic Leadership. Some of these zingers do apply to other leadership styles and concepts; but based on the author's experiences, these are the major ones that may help the reader in the quest for Synergetic Leadership success. Thus, without further ado...

1. So in everything, do to others what you would have them do to you, for this sums up the Law and the Prophets.
(Matthew 7:12, NIV) This is a common knowledge quote. There are many corollaries to this quote. One version for this quote is: "Treat others like you would like to be treated". Paradoxically, you can treat the statement in a negative sheen, such as "Don't do something you wouldn't want to be done to you." To assert the concept more personally, another corollary would be "Treat people the way you wish your loved ones would be treated." In any case, the standard of treatment expected is based on equitability, (read equality) between actors. In leadership, this equitability in treatment is between team members and the synergetic leader. Additionally, this zinger also applies to the treatment among the team members themselves. This quote does refer to the equal treatment between the synergetic leader and all the team members.

This particular biblical quote is remarkable in many ways. First of all, notice Jesus Himself is citing previously recorded data (Law and the Prophets). The lesson here is to understand you do not have to "re-invent the wheel" in a Synergetic Leadership environment. As a minimum, regardless of the contention of issues, a standard of fairness, cordiality, and respect is expected. (Respect will be addressed in a later zinger). Everyone listening to Jesus should have known the standard of behavior. When a synergetic construct is applied, dissenting opinions are just as valid as the axiom of the issue proposed. In order to ascertain the validity of the efforts of all team members, even the derived "non-applied" solutions need to be treated as a valid input to the desired goal, i.e., a possible solution. Doing so, allows all team members to openly and assertively engage in the tasks of synergy leadership applications. Therefore, treat all team inputs well, as you wish your input to be treated. Do this even when the treatment received bears no positive equitability to yours.

In addition, notice the plurality of this quote. It uses the words "others" and "them". This plurality has a synergetic angle to the treatment of others. There is an emphasis on the team (multiple individuals) interacting with other team members. Again, the standard of equal treatment, or equitability, is expected. This treatment asserts the validity of all team members' input towards the pursuit of solutions. In the military, the simple act of saluting each other while officers and enlisted pass by shows the equitability of treatment. Salutes are exchanged regardless of the disparity of rank in recognition of the plural effort of all military members towards the stated goal of the military.

This plurality also brings us back to the synergetic leader. The synergetic leader exchanges with the group and the group later take similar actions with the leader. This is important. If the standard of treatment from the leader to the team member does not meet the expected or understood standard of the team members, then the reverse may (and usually does) occur. The leader will receive substandard treatment, usually accompanied by substandard input to the confronted issues. The exchange between the synergetic leader and the team members must be in harmony with each other. Since the leader initiates the exchange, it is up to this individual to set the tone and expectations of the exchange between leadership and team members. A well delivery of treatment between the synergetic leaders and team members bodes well for the application of synergy and success. This is a quintessential expectation of a synergetic environment, which thus brings us to zinger #2, the team goals.

2. It is not about the leader, it's about the team goals. In general, among recorders of leadership actions, there seems to be a deep routed emphasis on the leader and not the leadership per se. Buttressing against Zinger #1, equitability centered synergy always points to (or emphasizes) the team and de-emphasizing the leader. Earlier cited General Colin Powell also asserted that to be successful in a leadership position, it helps to surround yourself with smart people. If you believe the notion each individual on a team is good or proficient in a specific area, then it is this team's member contribution, along with other contributions of other team members, which produces success. The leader himself is not the fulcrum. The fulcrum should be the team's stated goals and results, based on synergy.

It is about leadership, not the leader. (This idea will be addressed in-depth at a later zinger). The accomplishment of the team stands in the primacy over the leaders. A true leader, specifically a synergetic leader, understands this premise of the team's accomplishment over the leader's effort. The moment a leader lets the synergy center leadership processes, true team cohesion and success will be achieved. These accomplishments will be greater than the individual efforts could afford. Yet, we need to have a common intertwining attitude to deliver cohesion. Enter Zinger #3, the concept of team respect.

3. Synergy flourishes when multilateral respect is exercised.
The biblical quote used earlier (Mathew 7:12, NIV) referencing treatment is generally well understood. (Although not universally practiced). The standard of equitability is clearly defined. What is not clearly defined is what constitutes, or how this equitability is delivered. The basic starting point is respect. Respect is defined as giving someone (or something) higher esteem (than yourself). Thus, the individual practicing respect shows deference to the individual who is being respected. In mutual (or multilateral) respect, the same treatment then is returned. The receiver of respect returns the treatment to the individual who began the respectful exchange. The individuals are now in a position to accept each other in higher esteem,

and therefore should treat each other with equality. In this environment, the free exchange of ideas flourishes. The emphasis is on the ideas, not the individuals. In this construct, an environment of "doing what's right, no matter who's right" foments a synergetic solution to whatever issue is at hand. More on this concept will be expanded in the next zinger.

Notice that respect is not necessarily synonymous with congeniality. The latter is not required but may enhance synergy. Congeniality must not take precedence over synergy. Respectful synergetic exchanges between team members will provide the impetus for success.

In a Synergetic Leadership model there are, and always will be disagreements. There is a term for this condition, from the French. It is called détente. Even if not friendly with each other, different actors (team members) will work with each other to achieve a common goal. Under a respectful construct, a team member may agree to disagree with others, with no detriment to the team's cohesion. The synergetic leader maintains this cohesion by emphasizing the solution and de-emphasizing the discord of ideas. A good synergetic leader addresses the contraindicated behaviors and attitudes as a detour of stated goals, and when necessary will direct the solution emphasis, forcefully if needed, to ensure team success. This construct takes us to the next zinger. It relates to the measure of success.

4. It is not who's right, it is what's right. Common Knowledge quote. As mentioned before, a good synergetic leader de-emphasizes himself, so the team effort is emphasized. In addition, this concept is also true among team members. Under this philosophy, synergy is blind to the individual effort, in particular, the effort of the leader. Only the combined effort of the team members aggregates the best score.

This approach may sound simple but may seem contraindicated with some leaders and team members. Thus, this concept has to be taught and repeated constantly until it becomes part of the culture in a Synergetic Leadership environment. The problem is many individuals equate being right with what's right. This leads into a faulty logical sequence in which if an individual was right in the past, then by consequence the same will be true in the future. This is a fallacy. Many individual financial investors are aware of the notices on the disclaimers with financial institutions. This disclaimer asserts, that "past performance is no guarantee or indication of future results." In reality, no one knows what exactly the future brings, especially in the complex world of leadership constructs.

Therefore, in a Synergetic Leadership construct, the emphasis is on the right actions at a specific time to solve a specific situation. In other words, Synergetic Leadership provides the right action at that precise moment, regardless of who devised the solution. This solution will probably affect the thought processes and inclination of future decisions. Yet, in the next challenge, a different solution may be applied based on the new set of circumstances. There may be a new input from a different team member overshadowing a previously used input. This would make the previous other team members' ideas inconsequential. The important factor is the achievement of the desired outcome, and not who derived such action. This brings us to the next zinger, the "intelligence apex conundrum".

5. Assume at least one follower (team member) is as competent as you. Nurture this competence! At the risk of sounding "uber repetitive", a synergetic leader is not the one who always is, or should, be right. Following General Colin Powell's advice, a synergetic leader is benefited by surrounding himself with smart people. In fact, the smarter the better. A

174

synergistic leader brings "to the table" a facilitator methodology in problem-solving. The leader exposes the issue and then lets synergy derive the best possible outcome. The leader may not be the smartest individual in the room. In fact, the synergetic leader is probably not the apex of intelligence in the room. However, the synergetic leader brings the tools to extract the right answer to the issues. Again, it is not who's right (the leader or perhaps the smartest team member), its what's right (the synergetic solution achieved).

A successful synergistic leader will most likely work with and influence very intelligent people. If the leader has a team member with exceeding intelligence or other synergetic skills, then it is up to the synergetic leader to expose and nurture the vast human capital within this team member. It is imperative to allow this individual to show or prove the vast amount of available human capital available to the team. In synergy, you don't need to be the genius, you just have to find the best resources among the team. Sometimes these individuals can become frictional, in terms of the action to be taken or the delivery of the data in defiance. This brings us to the issue of team member defiance, our next zinger.

6. Defiance is not necessarily detrimental; the leader may be going the wrong way. It is common to hear individuals say, "I have a tough skin, you can't hurt me, call it like it is," etc. But it takes a synergetic leader who emphasizes the "what's right" concept completely enough to not be professionally or personally distraught with a defiant team member. This is especially true when the defiance is directly targeted to the leader's main point of view (regardless of which leadership style is practiced). Some leaders surmise defiance as a corruptive and dysfunctional influence on other team members. This may be true if the dissent is continuous and not supported by data. But organically, defiance is not necessarily a bad thing. Defiance makes the leader introspect the issue or course of action. The way synergy can be accomplished in a defiant moment is to remind all team members the team is searching what's right, not who's right. The defiant team member should then be encouraged to source the data required to make the point, understanding that saying "this is what I feel" normally does not carry the logical weight that actual researched data does.

Another positive aspect of defiance relates to defiance being a "last chance" input for the leader to ascertain the validity of a course of action. Remember, leadership constructs, to include Synergetic Leadership, allow the leader to override the defiant. Since the leader is responsible for the team's outcome, leadership always reserves the right of what action is to be chosen. (If defiance overrides the leader's decision, the problem is outside the scope of synergy or any leadership construct).

One last point about defiance. Never take defiance personally, nor berate the defiant. Today's defiant team member is tomorrow's synergetic contributor. If the discord is treated with professional respect, both parties will tend to gain from the experience. The defiant member will know discord is respected within the team, and the leader can benefit knowing at least one member is not afraid to "push back" on a particular issue. The attitude taken by both the leader and the defiant team member is crucial for the success of a defiant issue. The concept of attitude takes us to the next zinger.

7. Smiles and Frowns are like tuberculosis; all are equally contagious. Some leaders may not be able to or are not comfortable with presenting a positive attitude for a variety of reasons. If you are in this category, then: try harder! The interpersonal aspects of leadership demand interactivity with a diverse spectrum of team players. A positive outlook and having a positive demur are complementary. These, in turn, seems to act as a force multiplier in a Synergetic Leadership environment. A positive attitude does not equate to joviality, being funny or entertaining. A positive focus presumes the team is capable and can be willing to exercise their personal and professional efforts to meet and perhaps exceed the tasks or goals required. There is a common adage stating, "So goes the head, so goes the rest of the body." Since the choices between a positive attitude and a negative attitude are mutually exclusive, then a clear argument is made to make the led environment a positive experience for all involved.

This is not to say in the course of the day to day operations negative events or negative issues can be excluded from the team's environment. However, a synergetic leader should recognize this aberration, address it with team members affected, and emphasize the general environment redirection towards the positive side of the challenge.

Yet, common to most leadership models, the prevailing attitude of the entire team does begin (although is not necessarily centered), with the leader's demur and focus. This is an uncomfortable reality to some leaders, especially if two conditions appear, (either together or separately). First, are the leader's personal issues. A leader's negative issues, which should be temporary, need to be acknowledged by the leader, dealt with and resolved. In a synergetic team, the next leadership capable individual (in the team) may need to take over or supplement the need for positive focus for the team. This is why in Synergetic Leadership, you don't "go it alone." There is always a "deputy." The chosen "deputy" should continue the team's direction toward stated goal success."

The other main issue is personalities. The designated leader may not have a positive attitude infused personality.

177

This is not a dire situation as it may seem. What is required in this condition is the acknowledgment by the team of such a "non-positive" personality. This will probably be immediately apparent to the team since humans are sensitive to attitudes. Yet, if the leader is understood to be a trusted agent, willing to lead the team with synergy, then the focus becomes more about synergetic results and less on the negative proclivities of the leader.

If the negativity is a long-term issue, or the leader is incapable (or refuses) to address the lack of a positive focus on the team, then serious consideration of career roles is required. In a synergetic environment, everything possible to enhance a synergetic approach to leadership must be attempted. This starts with the correct positive focus of the leader.

The bottom line, and at the risk of sounding "nonchalant" about this subject, a leader needs to be positive and smile. Leaders should try to avoid behaving negatively. Remember, the team tends to reflect the attitude of its leader. A leader's attitude should be worth emulating. Furthermore, this focus is both directed to the team, and specifically to each team member. This leads us to the next zinger, the importance of the recognition of singularity.

8. Everyone is someone. Synergetic Leadership aggregates the individual input of a team. The key to Synergetic Leadership is, indeed, the synergy (process) which leads to the success of stated goals. In synergy, it is the individual cooperative effort and interest which achieves the stated goals. The center of Synergetic Leadership is group dynamics.

Importantly, group dynamics come from individual inputs. Normally, each input is brought forth by an individual. The contribution is individualized. Synergy presumes individuals working together. This individuality is to be recognized, and perhaps even better, cherished.

The way a synergistic leader nurtures aggregate success is to recognize individual contributions. You should not give a trophy for every input. But every input should be recognized. A quick note or an in-person specific thank you may motivate the team member to future recognizable efforts.

One way to do this is to remember two things. First is what was the notable input, and secondly who was responsible for the input. To do this, a leader must either know or be able to assertively find out, who was the input's contributor. The center of this premise is that a significant input from an individual should always be recognized. A simple verbal accolade can suffice, all the way to a formal award (depending on the relevance of the input). When possible, recognize the input with the team present. This mode gives value to the individual in the group.

A word of caution is necessary. This stated mode of individual recognition does not mean a constant deluge of pleasantries. Too much of a good thing can dilute its effectiveness. Positive remarks are always welcomed. But not every positive team input deserves a "Nobel Prize." A good synergetic leader will understand, based on the type and progress of the team, how much recognition is appropriate and when to acknowledge.

The important point to consider is the use of the real name or monikers of individuals, i.e. get to know the team. Show deference to people's individuality. Find what things team members enjoy, and why. There may be "mini-groups" inside the team. Therefore, you may need to find different, yet common, ground. No excuses! Find commonality with team members and share yourself with them. As has been stated before, nurture and mentor team members. This environment takes us to the opposite side of success, our next zinger.

9. By definition, leadership does not accept failures. Leadership only accepts temporary shortcomings towards imminent success. There is a difference between failures and unmet expectations. In Synergetic Leadership, failure is understood to be the anomaly of incorrect input. Theoretically, in a synergetic environment, the best outcome should arrive by matching the best input to the solution at hand. Notice the prior sentence begins with the word theoretically. In real life, the dynamics of measurable success is a constant juxtaposition of right and wrong answers to the teams' challenges toward the stated goals. Not only are mistakes and setbacks possible, but these are also a fact of the dynamics of leadership. This includes Synergetic Leadership as well. Sometimes, the team will fall "short" of achieving the stated goals.

Synergetic Leadership focuses on what can be done, not how things got "screwed up." What can act as a force multiplier in relation to success or failure of stated goals is the outcome of temporary undesirable results. Failure is not the end-all in Synergetic Leadership. A failure may mean a different leadership focus is required. The idea is to utilize a failure to correct the deficiency of the synergetic approach. Either the goal changed amid the timeframe given and the synergy was improperly applied (applied to the incorrect goal), or the synergetic input of the team was not addressing the stated goals. Either way, the required goals were not achieved. In this case, the self-correction of the team is required. Addressing the team deficiencies makes the attainable goals possible. The important takeaway that needs to be a failure is not accepted. Reversing whatever failure occurs becomes the positive effect of the problem.

The past 9 zingers discussed general approaches for successful Synergetic Leadership constructs. The next and final zinger sort of completes the general discussion of Synergetic Leadership. Oddly enough, it may sound like a bad misnomer, or perhaps a typographical mistake. It is not. Let's meet Lima Echo Cubed, or better known as **LE³·**

10. LE³ (Pronounced in its' alphanumerical format: Lima Echo Cubed). ***LE*adership is the *LE*gacy of the *LE*ader.** The legacy of the leader in the leadership style used, good or not so good. If you apply good leadership, your leadership will be remembered, perhaps emulated, even if the next set of leadership practitioners forget your name. This book makes the case for Synergetic Leadership. Synergetic leadership centers on the team, and its legacy enhances the stated goals, or goals to be met in the future.

There seems to be a cultural emphasis on the leader at the expense of the leadership style used. Media seem to focus on a specific leader most of the time. It appears society in general wants to praise the leader, and then understand what result the leader is being praised. Record-setting athletic achievements tend to reflect on the athlete at the expense of the coaches, team members, and trainers who helped towards the goal. The leader becomes the primary focus. The process appears secondary, and only important to academics who want to learn how the goals were achieved. This book makes the case completely backward, or in the better term, reverse logic. Notice **LE³** states the words leadership, legacy, and leader in this order purposely. Let's examine why.

Foremost, leadership styles should be set forth or left to ensure the benefit of the organization and the human experience in general. No matter what challenges the organization encounters, it is hoped there will be a leadership style that will help in the attenuation or resolution of problems and simultaneously accomplish the stated goals. This book attempts to make the case the goal of leadership is the "Opus Maximus" of the leader, and therefore the reason, for a leadership construct. The case for Synergetic Leadership is made as a "top tier" leadership style to accomplish this goal. Whether you are convinced or are "chomping at the bit" to argue against the Synergetic Leadership construct, the point is to assert an understanding of leadership styles. These leadership styles should help solve present and future organizational challenges, and benefit society in general.

The term legacy becomes the conduit between the leadership style, which was successful in asserting or completing the stated goals, and the leader. The leadership constructs left behind (legacy), or the attributed effort delivered, is accentuated for the purpose of continuous organizational success and the betterment of society in general. The legacy left behind does acknowledge the stewardship of the applicable leader. This leader is recognized for being able to produce positive results using the stated leadership style, or possibly multiple styles. (The complexity of the forum in which leadership was applied might have included multiple leadership styles).

Lastly, **LE³** does mention the leader. This connection between the leader and the leadership style left as a legacy is noteworthy. However, this connection should be no more than a mere data point. By comparison, leadership greatly overshadows the leader. The importance of the concept of leadership and its potential and application for the betterment of the human experience is far more relevant than the person who was successful in its' application.

Examples of **LE³** abound. Let's explore a poignant one. As you read this paragraph, no matter what day it is, or what time it is, there is a nuclear-powered US NAVY submarine, deep in an ocean, in international waters, protecting us and our way of life. The leader of this vessel is a captain. This individual has full authority over the ship and its crew. This individual is deprived of the things we take for granted. To feed the crew, he only has as much food as the vessel can carry. The medical facilities are limited in case of a medical issue on a crew member. Furthermore, every action (or lack thereof) taken will be measured against the highest standards of professionalism. Failure in leadership can certainly cause severe or deadly results.

Neither you nor I know this individual's name. What we do know if the standard which this individual is held, and the result (good or bad) which is delivered by the leadership applied.

Thus, the name of the submarine captain is not as important as what the vessel's leadership model is expected to accomplish. The success of this vessel is tied to the strategies and tactics learned throughout the history of naval operations, (in particular submarine warfare), and the stated goal of the mission attempted.

When this captain is relieved from duty, the mission, strategies, tactics and leadership models remain. This individual may add or help modify these models, but it is the institution that remains. In the case of leadership models, for the time he was in command, every leadership decision or action is taken will serve as a measurable standard to his crew. This measure may repeat itself when junior members of his crew raise to the level of leaders themselves. It is here where we find that the captain's contribution is the leadership he leaves. The captain is not the fulcrum of the legacy, it's the leadership he lives that should live on as part of the US NAVY.

The latter idea holds true for any teams involved. The impetus of Synergetic Leadership is to expose the teams' aggregate effort as a qualifier of the concept of leadership. This qualifier addresses the reason for success. The primacy is not centered around the leader or individual team members. It is centered around aggregate cooperation. Remember, the concept of synergetic leadership is based on "what's right", and not on "who's right."

The positive aspect of leadership on the human experience takes primacy over the leader or the team. Both the leader and/or the team leave a leadership style as a legacy, to help in the establishment of success to present and future stated goals. This success should be true for subsequent teams, and in continuum to the human experience in general. The remembrance of the leader should take the lowest tier of importance compared to the remembrance of the leadership delivered and left behind since the latter should be the constant leadership structure. What remains is the leadership style which nurtures success.

We started this chapter with "Hey batter batter, swing batter batter". If you play or enjoy baseball, I hope you smile every time a kid repeats this banter. Likewise, in Synergetic Leadership, I hope you remember some of these zingers. In particular, try to remember Matthew 7:12 and **LE^3**. The former will remind you of the standard of treatment of the team. The later will keep you humble and focused on the reason to be a leader.

Chapter 9

Conclusion

"That's all I got to say about that" from the movie Forrest Gump (Tom Hanks)

It is hoped this book has helped you in two ways. First and foremost, this book has advocated for a concise and usable definition of leadership. The concept of leadership is advocated to be the human application of synergy, i.e. **Human Applied Synergy**. Although other leadership constructs are practiced in nature, i.e. wolf packs, etc., the latter's application is simply for the survival of the species. In humans, leadership has been adapted to improve the quality of the human experience far beyond surviving and reproducing. Leadership conveys a set of principles and steps to make the human experience better in some way.

The reason for a concise and simple definition of leadership in this book is because academia continues to struggle with the definition of leadership. Academic professionals have tried to codify the definition and test this codification for appropriate validity. This process has led to specific measurable data points but has not simplified the definition. In some cases, the results of studies have created constructs with definitions more complex than the original axiom. These, in turn, leave the practitioner of leadership with an unusable standard.

This phenomenon is not particular to the concept of leadership. The reader may ponder what constitutes music, or art, or even wisdom? Perhaps any definition of any human construct is an enigma in itself. Yet, whether in the business world, military organization, or any institution where the desire for a better outcome better than the "status quo", the leader must apply some form of leadership. Therefore, the leadership practitioner must understand the concept of leadership at the most basic of levels, and then apply it successfully in their applicable forum. This leads us to the applicable concept of leadership.

The advocation for this book is a definition of leadership based on the concept of synergy. Synergy, as stated, is a force multiplier by nature. If you put more people towards the solution of a problem, the cooperative effort will produce a better result than the "status quo." To build a road between two cities takes much more than a cement truck. A myriad of engineers, architects, raw material suppliers and workers play a part in the accomplishment of the stated goal (the road). There needs to be synergy among all these individuals. This book has advocated a leadership construct attempting the same goals as the understood definition of synergy.

Recall that synergy is practiced by artificial intelligence systems. Machines do "cooperate" with other machines to produce a better product or service faster, more efficiently and of better quality. Yet this synergy is at the control of the programmers, the machine is only motivated by the energy power system applied. Synergetic Leadership is applied by human effort on other humans, attempting to achieve a better condition of the human experience in some form.

This book provides a starting point for a definition of leadership. At its most basic level, leadership's goal is to somehow improve the human condition. Which then begs the question: how do we accomplish such a goal? The answer is

186

somewhat unknown. This book fully acknowledges a synergetic leadership theory has not been put through the arduous tests of academic dissection. True as this may be, Synergetic Leadership is based on synergy, a concept with results which does not need further proof. The only part of the theory to prove is the connection between the application of synergy and how does this application relate to known styles of leadership.

The second way this book attempts to help the reader is by providing some answers to the practicability of Synergetic Leadership (Chapter 2). The narrative of this chapter applied and contrasted the term Synergetic Leadership with 30 leadership related terms for discussion. These commentaries can be the starting analysis of suitability for the term Synergetic Leadership.

Meanwhile, the leadership practitioner is left with a starting point to use a leadership style for the betterment of the practitioners' leadership environment. At the very least, the practitioner of leadership, using a synergetic measurement of progress, can measure the use of synergy to decide if the latter is the fulcrum of their respective leadership environment. If it is, the practitioner can ascertain the synergetic model is plausibly validated. If the synergy model is not validated, then the practitioner may find a more productive process when compared to the synergetic model.

If Synergetic Leadership did not provide the necessary improvements to the stated goals, then the leadership practitioner may now try a suitable alternate to synergy. This may produce an even better construct for the term leadership. In which case, the pursuit of the best type, and the understanding of leadership should be achieved. This is to be understood as a win-win situation.

Furthermore, there is no discourse in this book in opposition to academia in terms of how leadership is defined or the usable practicability of the term "leadership" as it pertains to the leadership practitioner. It is presumed academic centered individuals do practice leadership construct themselves. They have a vested interest for themselves to have the same tools and understanding of leadership to apply to their own leadership constructs. Academia mirrors other leadership practitioners. The challenge for the best answer to leadership is for everyone, including academics.

So where to go from here? The answer is simple and in the purview of academia. Synergetic Leadership must be tested against other leadership constructs. How? This is not simple. The challenge of the term leadership is sometimes defined by results and sometimes defined by the process. Even further, leadership can be defined by both methods mentioned. Perhaps the answer lays in synergy, which is a process to obtain optimum results. If leadership can be defined as a process, then whatever processes inside the spectrum of leadership can be tested against the known concept of synergy.

Finally, it is hoped this book has enriched you in a few ways. If nothing else, it is hoped the reader, and especially a leadership practitioner will now approach leadership as a synergetic process. This process alone, as alluded earlier, will produce a better result than if nothing else was attempted. If synergy is successful, the leadership practitioner can tailor her or his personal attributes to either improve the delivery of synergy, or improve the concept of Synergetic Leadership, or both. This would be a victory for all involved because leadership would be improved as a term, and as a result.

The challenge is for you to now approach your organizational leadership goals with synergy in mind and succeed! To this end, I hope this book has provided a valuable

188

tool for your use. Your author wishes success in your pursuit and employment of leadership.

Acknowledgments

My faith anchors my life. I give thanks to the Lord for allowing me the privilege of this journey. Without him, nothing is possible. By His grace, everything is achieved.

To my quad-**B** (**B**eautiful, **B**eloved, **B**adger {University of Wisconsin mascot}, **B**ride): thank you for all the moral support and encouragement. It would take the eloquence of a poet with the vocabulary of a dictionary to express my gratitude. You are the best, and I love you.

To my son Christopher and my daughter Elena, you are both an inspiration to me. Christopher, wherever you gather, you are usually the smartest individual in the room. I'm in awe of you always. Elena, you have inspired me many times. You were the first proofreader/editor of this book. You did a great job. Thank you and remember; there is no nobler endeavor than to be the advocate of a child.

To my mother Patricia (Pat) Sobrino (nee Speer), who was a thesis short in completing a Ph.D. in English. (The academic pursuit was cut short due to ovarian cancer, which took her life). You inspired me to be the best at whatever I tried. I miss you. To dad, Pedro Sobrino Marrero, who sacrificed so much, so my brother and I would have the right education for success. You showed us the importance of sacrificial love, and we got the message loud and clear. And to Pete, my brother; the best of times are spent with you, and a couple of cigars. You are great!

To Captain and Mrs. Lluesma, I owe so much. Don (Captain) Ernesto, little would you know the importance of your patient explanation of leadership to a child. I hope this book will meet with your approval. To "Profesora" Lluesma.

you were mom's closest friend, colleague, and ally. I thank you for your devoted friendship to Mom, and the patience it took to teach me Business English.

To my dear friend EdD Vince Hughes, you made me think of the possibilities of academic pursuits. You are a better leader than perhaps you give yourself credit. Thank you for being there for me. By the way, nice work editing and proofreading this book. No wonder they made you a Doctor of Education. Ditto to Mrs. Mary Hughes, thank you for volunteering your academic skills towards the effort!

To Karen Householder, you are the only author I ever met. Your proofreading and "beta" reading were outstanding. But the most valuable contribution was your insights on how to write and publish a book. Please consider yourself hugged!

To my former military commanders, Lt Cols Rennie and Dole and Lt Gen Lichte. It was my privilege to follow you and learn to be a leader. I do thank you deeply for the opportunity.

To the great officers and enlisted personnel who I shared the KC-10A schoolhouse at the 305 Operational Support Squadron, Combat Crew Training School, Barksdale, and McGuire Air Force Bases, LA & NJ. I learned a lot about leadership from you, especially from the senior enlisted personnel. Let's all remember …. life is too short to smoke cheap cigars (TSgt Pete Hatzinger, colleague, circa 1998).

Finally, but never last in my memories or in my heart, many thanks to the members of the 332nd Airlift Flight (Geographically Separated Unit of the 458 Airlift Squadron, Scott Air Force Base, IL), at Randolph AFB, TX. "Quis Custodiet Ipsos Custodes" (Juvenal). You all inspired me to be a better leader. You still do, always.

References

Abbott, B. & Costello, L. (1938), "Who's on First?", Kate's Smith Hour radio program, 24 Mar 1938.

Antonakis, J. & Day, D.V. (2018). *The Nature of Leadership* (Third Edition). Thousand Oaks, California. SAGE Publications.

Bible, International Standard Version (2011). *Judges, Chapter 7, verse 17*. Old Testament.

Bible, New International Standard Version (1984), *Matthew, Chapter 7, verse 12*. Grand Rapids, MI. Zondervan Publications.

Dolby, T. (1982), *She Blinded Me with Science*, Album: The Golden age of Wireless. United Kingdom.

Golding, W. (2006), *The Lord of the Flies, a novel*. New York: Perigee, 1954.

Hanks, T. (1994), *Forrest Gump*, written by Eric Roth, based on the novel by Groom, W.

Juvenal, D.L.L. (I Century A.D.), *Satire VI*, Lines 347-348.

Truman, Harry S. (n.d.). BrainyQuotes.com. Retrieved June 30, 2019, from BrainyQuote.com Web site: Https://www.braineyquote.com/quotes/harry_s_truman_109615

Yogi Berra Quotes (n.d.). BrainyQuotes.com. Retrieved June 22, 2019, from BrainyQuote.com Web site: https://brainyquote.com/quotes/yogi_berra_380870

Index

ABOUT THE AUTHOR: David "Ricky" Sobrino was born and grew up near San Juan, Puerto Rico. He studied Hospitality Management, finishing an undergraduate degree at Florida International University, Miami, FL. After a short career in the hospitality business, David joined the United States Air Force as a pilot. He served at first as a helicopter pilot and then transitioned to become an airplane pilot. He would later complete a master's in human resource management while in his military career. Through a 20-year career, he served in many capacities, including as a commander of a flying unit. The practical applications of leadership are his passion. It has been a life-long quest to understand the human application of the concept of leadership. This book encompasses the practice of leadership, learned after 40+ years of curiosity, study, analysis, and applications. Although this book is his maiden effort, he already has plans for more titles related to the subject of leadership. He currently lives in the mid-west. For questions or comments about leadership, David can be reached at Rickyleadership@writeme.com.